The More
the Merrier

Book 4

A Novel By
D. Thrush

Cover design by Bukovero
Title page art courtesy of Clipart
Drawings by D. Thrush

ASIN: B077Z7TJ9D
ISBN-10: 1981470166
ISBN-13: 978-1981470167

Praise for *The More the Merrier!*

"Great finish!" Kayla Merta

"Fun, funny and romantic... It really doesn't have to be Christmas to enjoy this magical series of books." constant reader

"Wow! I really enjoyed these series... Thanks for such a wonderful read." Redhearts

"This is a fun series. The only bad thing about this one is it is supposed to be the final one. We need more stories about the Claus family." David Reese

"What a great ending to this series. I loved how everything came together..." Kindle Customer

"I loved this series and this final book did not change that. Santina is one tough cookie!" Georgianna Miller

"I read the entire series and was thrilled with them. The stories are cute and perfect for the season..." Kindle Customer

"Loved all 4 of them couldn't put them down..." Maggie Muir

"...I have loved all four books and will definitely be reading more by this author." Linda

"What a whirl wind of emotions. Sad that this series has come to an end, but what a great ending!" Kayla

Novels by D. Thrush

Chick Lit / Rom Com

The Santa Secret (Prequel)
The Daughter Claus (Book 1)
The Claus Cause (Book 2)
Merrily Ever After (Book 3)
The More the Merrier (Book 4)

Fairy Tale Karma

~*~*~*~*~*~*~*~*~*~*~

Literary & Women's Fiction

Guardian of the Light

Whims & Vices (Book 1)
Fate & Flirtations (Book 2)

All the Little Secrets (Book 1)
Little Secrets Revealed (Book 2)

~*~*~*~*~*~*~*~*~*~*~

Contents

1 *Nut Job*

Santina Claus opened her eyes and stretched. What time was it? She glanced at the clock. Good. It wasn't too late. She was alone in bed and turned to look out the large window. It was another beautiful, sunny day. A gentle breeze fluttered the lacy curtains, and she heard the faint sound of a guitar. It made her smile as she threw back the covers and jumped out of bed. But first, a trip to the bathroom.

George came in as she stood in front of the mirror, braiding her long hair. He wrapped his arms around her from behind, and she looked at their reflection in the mirror. His long dark hair contrasted with her white hair. Together, they were striking. No wonder people stared at them.

"Hello, wife." He kissed her shoulder.

"Hello, husband." She turned to give him a kiss. "I should just let your sister braid my hair when she gets here since she likes to do it, and it's easier than braiding it myself."

"Are you sure you want to tell her, Tina?"

She sighed, releasing him, and he followed her back into the bedroom where they began making the bed.

"I don't know. I never thought this far ahead, but I don't see how we can keep it from her much longer."

"I know. Gemma is persistent. She's the one who asks questions and wants to visit us in the winter."

"But if we tell her, could she keep a secret? She won't tell your brother or your parents when she goes back to Boston, will she?" Tina stood, holding a pillow.

"I think she can keep a secret, but I hate to put her in that position."

Tina sat on the bed. "I wish I could tell your grandmother. I love Grandma Grace."

"G.G. loves you too, and she'd sure get a kick out of it." He sat beside her. "So would my mother. You know how much she loves Christmas."

"Yes." Tina sighed again. "I always thought I'd marry somebody from the North Pole. I never imagined I'd have to hide who I am from my in-laws."

"You thought you'd marry Kai," George stated.

Tina shrugged. "There were other boys I dated, but I always thought..." She bit her lip. "When I came to Florida to go to college, I never intended to go back. I wanted to get away from my childhood and have my own life. I never thought I'd end up back home running the toy shop while the man I love is in Florida." She put her hand on his face. "I married the right guy and I'm so lucky."

"I'm the lucky one." George kissed her lightly. "I'm sorry you couldn't have the wedding you wanted."

"Oh, our wedding was perfect, George." Tina smiled. "You'll see what a Winter White wedding is like when we go to Kai and Sonia's wedding. It's funny. Everybody here wants a June wedding, but up there everyone wants a November wedding."

"Is your brother going?"

"I'm sure Nick will go. We grew up with Kai, but he won't be able to bring Isabella because she doesn't know who we are."

"I wonder how serious it is between them."

"Who knows what's going on with them? First, it was about publicity and now who knows?"

"I still can't believe my father-in-law is Santa Claus." George shook his head. "And I can't figure out what to call him. I mean, I can't call him Santa or Mr. Claus out in public, and I don't want to call him Nick because that's your brother's name."

"You should probably just call him Grumpy." Tina giggled and put her hand to her mouth.

"At least I can just call your mother Clara."

"Do you think your mother read that article in *Modern Woman's World* magazine about me a few months ago?" Tina wondered.

"I don't think she reads a lot of magazines."

"I guess it's lucky that most people took it as a joke.

I don't know why I ever did that interview. What was I thinking?" Tina shook her head at herself. "I'd better get dressed. Your sister will be here soon."

"And then there's the matter of giving our parents grandchildren." George grinned and pulled her to him. "We've been married almost a year. We should at least make the effort."

Tina squirmed away from him. "Not so fast. We don't even live in the same place half the time. How could we raise a family?"

"We'll figure it out."

"That's way in the future. Anyway, I'll be heading back up north soon and you'll be going out on tour." Tina opened the closet.

George groaned. "It seems like we're either rehearsing, touring, or in the studio recording."

"That's called success, silly husband."

"I'm not complaining. I just hate being apart."

"Me too." She held up a sundress. "What do you think?"

"Everything looks good on you."

"I'm serious."

"So am I."

"I never got to wear stuff like this at the North Pole. I love pastel colors." Tina turned to him. "Are you going to change?"

George looked down at his shorts and *Black Ice* T-shirt.

"What for? It's just my sister."

***

"I wish I had hair like yours," Gemma commented as she braided Tina's hair. "Mine is too thick and curly. I just have to let it do what it wants."

"I wish I had hair like yours," Tina responded. "Mine is too straight."

"But it's so silky. I just love the feel of it and the white color is amazing. Nobody has hair this color except your brother and older people."

"I think it makes me look pale," Tina confessed.

"Not at all. It makes you look... delicate."

"Do you like the scones?" George asked.

"You know I love your scones." Gemma popped a piece into her mouth. "I have no talent for baking or cooking like my brothers. Isn't that funny?" she said to Tina.

"Are you seeing Loren later?" Tina asked.

"After band rehearsal." Gemma's eyes flicked to her brother. "What time do you think you guys will finish?"

"I don't know. We're having a band meeting first," George answered. "It depends on whether Nick and Loren start debating about something."

"I thought they were getting along now," Tina said.

"Well, they're not fighting over Isabella anymore, but they still seem to disagree a lot."

"Do you think Loren still likes her?" Gemma asked casually.

"He only flirted with her to annoy Nick," Tina assured her. "He's totally into you."

"I don't like playing games." Gemma frowned.

"I've never seen him like this before and I've known him a long time," George said.

"Good." Gemma smiled and finished braiding Tina's hair. "All done." She broke off another piece of her scone. "So when is *Black Ice* going back out on tour? Loren wasn't sure."

"We're waiting to hear from our manager, Robin, about that. He'll be at the meeting, so we might find out tonight."

He gave Tina a surreptitious look, and she shook her head slightly.

"Do you want something to drink?" he asked Gemma.

"Just some water."

"We'll be right back." He took Tina's hand and pulled her into the kitchen. "Don't you want to tell her?" he asked in a hushed tone.

"I want to tell her. I really do. It's just going to open up a bunch of questions and she'll be thinking about it all night and she'll have to keep it from Loren," Tina reasoned. "Maybe we should wait until tomorrow."

"Let's just tell her. I trust her. She won't tell him if we ask her not to."

"I don't want to put her in that position..."

Gemma entered the kitchen. "What's going on? What aren't you telling me?"

"I... Are you working on a new book yet?" Tina deflected her attention.

Suddenly Gemma beamed. "Oh, my God! You're pregnant! I swear I won't tell anybody. When are you due?"

Tina blushed and quickly shook her head. "No. I just... I really want to know about your new book."

"Bummer."

Gemma spun and headed back into the living room. She sat cross-legged on the brown fabric couch.

"I'm not sure what I want to work on next. I want to write something a little different, you know?"

"Uh huh." Tina sat on the couch, relieved that the subject had changed.

"Do you guys want a smoothie? We have a mango and a pineapple," George offered.

"Sounds good." Tina nodded.

"Mom told me about something interesting she read," Gemma continued. "It sounds pretty crazy, but it might make a good book."

"What is it?" Tina asked, picking at a scone.

"I could probably take the basic idea and make it into something interesting," Gemma mused. "You won't believe it, though."

"What?" Tina smiled.

"It was an article in a magazine. It's about a woman who believes she's Santa's daughter." Gemma laughed.

George froze on his way to the kitchen. He turned back slowly.

"I guess it was on the news too, and the reporter

who wrote it said it was true, but, of course, it was a joke." Gemma shook her head. "The woman was obviously a nut job, but it might make a good story if I can figure out an angle. What do you think?"

"I don't think she's a nut job," Tina responded hesitantly. "How do we know what's true and what's not? Just because we don't know about something doesn't mean it's not true."

"Tina," George said. "Just tell her."

"Tell me what? Why are you guys acting so weird?" Gemma demanded. "You're not telling me something."

Tina cleared her throat. "It's awful that people don't believe anymore. Children believe. Your little nephew, Evan, believes. But there's so much cynicism. It just makes me so sad..."

George sat on the ottoman and took Tina's hand as he met Gemma's eyes. "I didn't believe it at first either. I had to see it for myself, but I've been there and it's all true."

"What are you talking about?" Gemma looked from one to the other.

"You can't tell anybody," Tina stressed. "Not your family and not Loren. Obviously, George and Nick know, but you see what happens when it gets out. People either think we're crazy or they stalk us. I shouldn't have done that interview." She shook her head. "I thought with all the bad news and negativity in the world that people needed something good..."

"You guys are totally messing with me," Gemma accused.

"No, we're not," George claimed. "This is going to totally blow your mind. Tina is..."

"It's me," Tina said. "I'm the nut job."

2 *With Gravy*

Santa sat in his recliner chair, clicking the remote. He kept clicking until he dropped it on the folding tray beside him with exasperation.

Clara looked up from the small desk where she was typing on her laptop. "What's wrong?"

"This stupid remote doesn't work," he grumbled.

"Maybe it needs batteries."

"I don't know where they are."

"They're in the kitchen drawer."

He fidgeted with impatience.

"Well, go get them. You have legs. You have to get up now and then, dear." She ran her fingers through her short white hair. "Have you shaved today? If you're not careful, your beard and mustache will grow back and people will recognize you."

Santa got up and stretched his back.

"You know, it's not good to be so sedentary. You remember what the doctor said after your heart attack. Do you want to take a walk or do something?"

"I'll go golfing with Marty when they get back from vacation."

"I don't know why you didn't want to go on that cruise with Marty and Myra. It would've been fun."

He waved his hand at her. "We see them almost every day. It would've been the same thing, just on a boat."

"It would do us some good to go out and do things."

"Like what?"

"Like traveling, for instance. Isn't there anywhere you want to go?" she asked.

"I've been everywhere."

"But that was for work, and I haven't been all over the world like you. We could see the sights together. Wouldn't that be fun?"

Santa went into the kitchen and Clara could hear him rummaging around in the drawer.

"What size batteries?" he called.

"Didn't you look? I think they're triple A."

He returned to the living room and picked up the remote to change the batteries.

"You miss it. That's the problem, isn't it?"

"Nah."

"Yes, you do. You didn't really want to retire yet. You weren't ready." Clara lowered her glasses to look at him.

"I had a good ten years or so left in me." Santa sat down heavily in the chair. "But Tina's in charge now. It's done."

"It never would've happened if you hadn't had your heart attack," Clara said. "But we could go back if that's what you want. It would work out for everyone. Then Tina could finish college and be here in Florida with George."

"Tina changed everything. I wouldn't know what to do anymore," he groused.

"Don't be silly. Besides, Walter could help you."

"Walter has been a good foreman for the United North Pole Workers and a good friend all these years."

"We couldn't have managed without him." Clara acknowledged. "He helped Tina adjust when she first took over and he could help you, too."

"I don't need him training me like some new hire."

"Don't be so stubborn. Do you want me to talk to Tina?"

"No. Except for a few problems, she's done a good job," he said. "I wish she hadn't gone crazy changing the way we do everything, though."

"She made a lot of improvements that were long overdue," Clara stated.

"Well, it's not like things were falling apart," he said defensively.

"Of course not, dear. But she's very efficient and things are running more smoothly."

"Things were just fine when I was running the North Pole," he asserted.

"Of course. I just meant... You should be proud of her."

"I am proud of her." He pounded his fist on his tray for emphasis.

"I don't think it's a good idea for you to go back. You get stressed out just talking about it." Clara pursed her lips.

"Why does everybody always think I have a problem with stress?" he yelled.

Clara turned back to her computer. "I'm inviting everyone over for dinner. I'm going to make George's veggie casserole."

"With gravy?" Santa asked hopefully. "Make lots of gravy."

***

"Are we lost again?" Lisa fretted. She gathered her reddish-brown hair into a ponytail. "Why don't they have any street signs here? And if they do, they're in Spanish."

"That's because we're in Costa Rica," Walter answered patiently. "We're not lost. I'll find the way. Try that road."

Lisa was driving because, as an elf, Walter was too short.

"But look at all the potholes," she protested.

"That's why we have four-wheel drive."

"I'm pulling over. Let's look at the map they gave us at the rental car place again."

She stopped the car along the narrow side of the road, not that they were blocking any other vehicles.

"You've been complaining since we got here," Walter said. "Don't you want to look at this house for sale? Then we'll have our own place when we visit every year and we'll be able to retire here someday."

"Yeah, but I can't even get cell service sometimes."

"I thought you loved it here as much as I do."

"I do love it," Lisa said. "It's beautiful. I love all the

birds and sitting on the beach…"

"But," he said.

"But why can't we just buy a place in Florida like Tina and George?"

"For one, it's more expensive, and it's not as…" He scanned the scenery. "…secluded and untamed. Look at this place. It's paradise."

"I saw a scorpion today and a huge bug that I don't even know what it was," she reminded him.

"No place is perfect."

"But I want to be close to Tina. She's my bestie."

"You're her assistant. You see her every day at the North Pole when we're working. It's nice for us to have some time alone away from work," he reasoned.

"That's fine for now, but what happens when you want to retire? We'll be away from everyone."

"They'll just have to come and visit us," he said cheerfully.

"But…"

"Florida is too crowded and expensive. And everyone stares at me."

"I know." Lisa gave him a sympathetic look. "I guess I'd just rather be closer to everyone. You'd get to see Santa and Clara in Florida and we could go out and see Nick's band and hang out with Tina and George. You like George."

"Of course I like George, but I thought we'd already decided this."

"I'm homesick," she whimpered.

"For the North Pole?"

"For our friends."

"Lisa," Walter said patiently. "I'm not going to retire for a long time, and once I do, we could go visit everyone in Florida anytime you want. We'll just live here for the rest of the time."

"Can I think about it?"

"Sure. Let's just go look at this property. Okay?"

"I'm sorry I'm being such a pain, Walter. I really am. You know I love you and want to be with you. I just feel like this is moving too fast."

"The same thing happened when we moved in together. You panicked," he said. "We can take things slower. I won't buy a place if you're not sure about it, but let's look at a few while we're here, okay? We might find one that you really like."

"What if you like it and I don't? I really don't like the bugs here." Lisa wrinkled her nose.

"Let's cross that bridge when we come to it." Walter peered at the map. "Go right. No, left."

***

"Nicky," Isabella murmured into the phone.

Why did he go weak when he heard her voice? He mumbled a response.

"Aren't you happy to hear from me?" she teased.

Nick was determined not to let her manipulate him like she'd done last year when she'd convinced him to play up their relationship for publicity, especially since there was no relationship, just a professional one. Though he had to concede the PR had been good for both their bands. But he wasn't going to admit that to her.

"Nick?"

"I'm here." He played with a loose thread on the hem of his shirt.

"You know who you remind me of?"

"Who?"

"Billy Idol."

"Billy Idol? I'm not punk," he scoffed.

"Yeah, but you have that white spiky hair and that same attitude."

"What attitude?"

"You know, rebellious, intense..."

"He's not like me at all," Nick interrupted.

"I used to have a big crush on him," she confessed.

"I get it. He's a lot like me, but I'm a lot more like me."

"You're funny." Isabella gave a little musical laugh. "What made you get into music?"

"I don't know. I couldn't stop making up songs and drumming on the toy drums in the toy shop... I mean my family's toy company."

Whew! He had to watch what he said.

"You know why I got into music?" She didn't wait for him to respond. "My mother was into musicals. I probably saw every old musical there is. She used to play the soundtracks. I bet I still know all the words to those old songs." She laughed lightly.

"Yeah? Which ones?" Nick wasn't familiar with those old movies, but he could listen to her melodious voice forever.

"I still get chills when I watch that scene in *Singin' in the Rain* when Gene Kelly dances in the rain because he's in love. It's so romantic." Isabella sighed. "And I love *The Music Man* and *West Side Story* and the song 'Matchmaker' with the three daughters in *Fiddler on the Roof*. Classics. Have you seen them?"

"Nah."

"Oh, Nicky, you're missing out."

"I'm not into the past."

"You should come over and we'll watch some of these movies together and you'll see how amazing they are," she enthused. "Really. It'll open up a whole new musical genre for you."

"Right."

Nick remembered the last time he'd gone to her house. She'd invited him for dinner and they'd ended up making out on the couch, but, as usual, she'd reminded him of her "rule." She didn't get involved with other musicians. Since then, he'd avoided her because he couldn't resist her. She had some kind of witchy power over him.

"Nick?"

"Huh?"

"I want you to come over and watch a musical with me. Will you do that for me?" Isabella asked.

"Okay."

Nick couldn't say no to her. Soon they'd be out on tour again and he wouldn't be able to avoid her, anyway. What did she want from him? Did she get some kind of sick thrill from teasing him? It didn't matter. He couldn't wait to see her again and was glad she had called him. That way, it wasn't his fault. After all, he didn't want to be rude.

3 *Speaking of Work*

"That's not funny, you guys." Gemma tucked her legs underneath herself on the couch. "Obviously, the poor woman who thinks she's Santa's daughter is delusional unless she was trying to get attention or... who knows?"

Tina and George exchanged looks.

"Quit messing with me," Gemma demanded.

"Did you notice how quickly Evan got attached to Tina?" George asked.

"What does that have to do with anything? Our nephew is four."

"Kids know," Tina said. "They sense it. The same thing always happened to my father when he was out in public. Little kids were drawn to him. He'd end up with a little parade behind him."

George smiled. "I can imagine."

"Okay. Very funny." Gemma rolled her eyes.

"It's a toy company way up north," George said slowly. "Think about it. You met Tina's parents. Didn't you feel a tiny bit of recognition with them?"

"How could I? I've never met them before."

"Yeah, but deep down, the child within you recognized them. Didn't you get a familiar feeling around them?" he persisted.

"Stop it, George."

"Seriously, when I found out, it all made sense. I knew it was true right away," he said.

"You did?" Tina asked.

"Things just fell into place," he told her. "All the secrecy, Nick's aversion to Christmas, your white hair, your evasiveness about where you lived up north..."

"Okay. Ha. Ha." Gemma frowned.

"I didn't think she'd react like this," Tina said to George. "I guess most people find it hard to believe."

"Walter," George blurted. "Walter is an elf. He's the foreman of the United North Pole Workers. He was at the wedding."

"That short guy with your friend Lisa?" Gemma asked.

"Yes, and Lisa is my assistant at the North Pole," Tina added.

Gemma shook her head. "You guys are really having fun with this, aren't you?"

"Okay, don't believe it." George waved his hand at her. "You'll see for yourself when you visit us."

"Just promise you won't mention this to anybody else," Tina said. "We have to remain anonymous."

"Sure you do." Gemma nodded. "Okay, so tell me, are the reindeer real?"

"Of course," Tina answered. "They guide the sleigh every year when I do the delivery."

"It's incredible. You should see it when she takes off into the sky," George marveled.

"Name all the reindeer." Gemma folded her arms.

"Why?" Tina asked.

"She's testing you," George said. "Just tell her."

"Okay. Blitzen considers himself the head reindeer..."

"I thought that was Rudolph," Gemma interjected.

"He'd love that, but no, it's Blitzen. Then Donner is sort of second in command. Rudy—I mean, Rudolph— likes to do karaoke. Then there's Dancer and Prancer, Dasher and Comet and Cupid. Oh, and Vixen."

"Okay, so you know the poem," Gemma said.

"What poem?"

"You know, 'Twas the Night Before Christmas.' It names all the reindeer," Gemma said. "Anyway, it might make a good book if I can figure out an angle."

"It doesn't matter," George said to Tina. "She'll find out soon enough when she visits."

***

"Lilliana is so hot," Kris said.

Nick nodded, not really listening. His thoughts were

consumed by Isabella as they stared at the TV in his living room.

"Wouldn't it be cool if I got together with Lilliana?" Kris asked. "Then we'd be dating sisters, and we'd be related."

Nick shook his head. "Isabella and Lilliana aren't sisters. They're just in *Rock Goddess* together. Besides, we're already related. We're cousins."

"Oh, yeah." Kris stroked his goatee. "I bet people think we're brothers because we both have white hair."

Nick hoped not. Kris was a little embarrassing at times, but at least he was a willing assistant and roadie.

"Our fathers look the same, except mine looks more like Santa since yours shaved," Kris remarked.

Santa didn't want to be recognized now that he was retired. Kris Kringle and Santa looked almost identical. Santa was the older sibling and a little shorter. They were both obstinate and brusque and competitive.

"I could've been Santa," Kris boasted. "But working with *Black Ice* is way more fun. And now we get to hang out all the time."

"Right."

"I still think it's wrong for Santa to be a girl. It's against nature or something."

"Huh?" Nick tuned into what he was saying. "Get woke, Kris. Tina's into it. It's her thing, and she's rocking it."

"How hard can it be if a girl can do it?" Kris commented.

Nick shook his head while he channel-surfed.

"It's no big deal. You just tell everybody what to do and sit in your office." Kris shrugged. "Sounds boring."

"It's high-pressure, man," Nick said. "That's why my father had a heart attack. He was always stressed out. I don't get the appeal of the job."

"We're lucky we got away from all that." Kris nodded. "Call Isabella and let's double date."

"No way."

"Why not? Set me up with Lilliana. We're perfect for

each other."

Nick grimaced. Kris was clueless. Lilliana was way out of his league. If anybody was perfect for anybody, it was Isabella for him. The aesthetic was perfect. Two rock stars rocking into the sunset. If only she could see it, too.

***

"I'm sorry, Walter. It's a beautiful place. Really," Lisa said.

Walter paced in their cottage. "I thought we talked about all this and you were on board."

"I am. I'd love to retire with you. Eventually," she insisted. "It's just the more I think about it, the more I realize that I'd rather be closer to everyone."

"It's less crowded here and less expensive. We can afford a much nicer place here."

"I know, but Tina's my best friend, and when would we ever get a chance to see everyone?" Lisa adjusted her ponytail.

"Before we met, I was just going to buy one of these little cottages. That's enough for me." Walter stood in front of the open sliding glass door, gazing out at the palm trees.

"Wouldn't you miss everyone? Admit it, Walter."

"I like the solitude here. It's low-key and peaceful."

"I love it here too, but after a while, it'd get boring."

"I'd never get bored here."

"But if we were in Florida, we could go out and see the band and you could see Santa and Clara and... there'd just be more to do."

"I don't need more to do. I need less to do." He turned to face her.

"Oh, Walter. I'm sorry. I totally get it. You're burned out. You like to get away from everyone. I guess I'm not there yet."

"No, *I'm* sorry, Lisa." He looked down and then back up at her. "You're more social. You like to go out and do things and see everyone. I hold you back from having fun."

"That's not true at all. We just have a classic extrovert-introvert dilemma." Lisa gasped. "Do you think that's it? Opposites attract. We're totally opposite."

"That's an exaggeration. We're not that different."

"Walter, think about it. You're male. I'm female. You're short. I'm... taller. You're older. I'm younger. You're an early riser. I like to sleep in. You like things tidy. I don't care. You're an elf. I'm... not."

"Well, when you put it that way..." He sighed.

"It's not a bad thing, but that explains why we've had a tough time adjusting to each other."

Lisa plopped down on the bed, and Walter sat beside her. "Is there hope for us?"

"Of course there is. We're perfect for each other." She grinned.

"I bet you were a good school counselor," Walter said.

"No. I was a terrible counselor. I couldn't be detached like you're supposed to be, and my own life was a mess. But that's how I met Tina." She smiled. "And you."

"So what do we do, counselor?"

"Buy two places?"

"We can't afford that."

"I know." Lisa sighed.

***

"Hi, Mom," Tina answered her phone.

"Hi. I just thought I'd invite everyone over for dinner one of these nights. What works for you?"

"Oh, George's sister, Gemma, is visiting." Tina glanced at Gemma, who was sitting at the dining table on her laptop.

"Okay. We'd better wait till she leaves since she doesn't know who we are. Even though she met us at the wedding, it's probably not a good idea," Clara said. "We have lots of time before you have to go back north."

"Yes. That sounds better. How are you and Dad?"

"You know your father. He's bored since Myra and Marty are on their cruise and he can't go golfing. I don't get the big thrill of golfing, but that's what they like to do. I wonder if they really sit in the bar most of the time. Hmm. I'd never thought of that before. But he watches it on TV, so maybe they really are golf fanatics."

"I thought you were going on the cruise with them," Tina said.

"I did too. But your father didn't want to go. I don't understand retiring if he never wants to do anything but play golf with Marty," Clara griped. "It's a good thing I have my own interests, but I thought we'd do a little traveling at least."

"Maybe in a few years."

"Maybe. Anyway, how's my wonderful son-in-law?"

"George is at rehearsal." Tina wandered into the bedroom and shut the door so Gemma couldn't overhear her. "I think I told you that Loren and Gemma like each other, so they're going to meet later."

"I just can't keep up with this stuff. It's such a soap opera." Clara gave a little laugh. "Have you talked to Walter and Lisa?"

"They're having trouble with their cell phone signal this year, so we mostly email. They've been looking at places over there."

"Goodness. I hope Walter isn't planning on retiring yet."

"He's just planning ahead, I think."

"Well then, good for him. He always loved it there."

"Funny to think of them being so far away," Tina said. "That would be weird."

"Speaking of work," Clara said. "You know your father really enjoyed going up to the North Pole and helping you out last year."

"That's great."

"When he was busy running the company, he didn't

have many opportunities to work with some of the departments, and I think he really got a kick out of it."

"I'm glad to hear that," Tina said.

"I think he especially enjoyed working in the mailroom and reading the letters. It reminded him of how rewarding it was. It just warmed his heart. You know what a big softie your father is."

"You guys are welcome anytime. I can always use the help, especially at the end of the season. You remember how busy it gets."

"That it does." Clara cleared her throat. "I have to admit, I've always felt bad about forcing you to take over the business."

"I was happy to do it, Mom. It was terrible when Dad had his heart attack and I didn't mind stepping in."

"Now, Tina, it wasn't fair to you. Your brother was the one who was supposed to take over," Clara said.

"It's fine. Things were happening for Nick's band, and I didn't expect him to give up his dreams."

"But you were in the middle of college. You had to give up *your* dreams."

"It all worked out. Once I got here, I realized how right it felt. Besides, the family history revealed that Santa was originally supposed to be a woman anyway, so everything turned out the way it was supposed to."

"But don't you want to go back to college and finish your education like you planned?" Clara asked.

"I can take online classes if I want, and I don't really need my degree anymore. I just like being up on the latest in business and technology."

"Nobody would blame you, Tina, if you moved back here to continue college and be with your husband. I know it's difficult for you and George to be separated for so long and I would completely understand if..."

"Even if I wanted to, how could I do that? Who would..."

"I don't think your father would mind coming back for a few more seasons. Just until you finish college," Clara assured her.

"Did Dad say he wants to come back?" Tina felt a bit of panic rise in her throat.

"No, he didn't. Not in so many words, but I'm sure he would if that's what you want. I'm just saying..."

"I appreciate the offer, Mom," Tina said. "I really do. You're right. I hate being away from my husband." A little thrill ran through her every time she called him that. "But I really do love running the company. Is it selfish to choose my career over being with George all the time?"

"Goodness, no, sweetie. Nobody thinks that's what you're doing. You can't look at it that way. George is on the road a lot, but that doesn't mean he's choosing his career over you. How did we get into all this?" Clara asked. "I just wanted to give you an option. That's all. You don't have to feel obligated to run the company anymore. That's all I wanted to say."

"Oh, Mom. It's not an obligation at all. I think this is what I was meant to do," Tina stated. "I know Dad's a little bored and you want me to involve him more, so he can come up and help anytime he wants, but there's no need for him to take over again. I've got it under control."

After they hung up, Tina noticed that her heart was beating a little faster. She sat down on the bed and put her head in her hands. It sure would be nice to be here in Florida all the time with George. But she couldn't imagine not returning to the North Pole. It still felt like home, and she'd miss working with Lisa and Walter. Why couldn't she have both?

4 *Musical Mood*

"Did you give Gemma a key so she can get in later?" Tina turned off the light in the bedroom.

"Yeah. But who knows whether she'll come back. She might stay at Loren's." George yawned.

Tina got into bed and cuddled up to him. "Do you think she will?"

"I don't know."

"It's funny that she didn't believe us. That never even occurred to me."

"Most people would probably think it's a joke."

"Really?"

Tina considered that. Why did so many people have trouble believing?

"Nick said your mother wants to have everybody over for dinner soon."

"Yes, once Gemma leaves."

"What difference does it make if we already told her?" he asked. "Meeting your parents might convince her."

"We can't tell my parents that we told her. They wouldn't be happy about it. They think our family should be anonymous and they're probably right. The interview I did last year didn't turn out like I thought it would."

Tina sat up as thoughts rolled around in her head. George bunched up his pillow and leaned back against it.

"You had good intentions. You just wanted to give people something positive to believe in," he said.

"I know, but people thought it was a big joke and I think my parents are right that if people knew about us, it would turn the North Pole into a tourist attraction. It would ruin it."

"That's probably true," he agreed.

"We can't tell my parents that we told Gemma, even though she doesn't believe us. And now she thinks I'm crazy."

"Don't worry about it."

"You don't think she'll tell *your* parents, do you?" The thought suddenly occurred to her.

"I don't think so. Guess we'd better tell her not to."

"Oh, my gosh! How do I get myself into these things?"

Tina got up and paced. She wore a large black T-shirt with the words *Black Ice* in light gray letters dripping like icicles. She could almost see the design in the dim light coming through the window.

"I'll talk to her tomorrow," George offered.

"My parents said people don't believe unless they're ready. We probably shouldn't have told her."

"We had to. She wants to visit us up north."

Tina stood before the window and stared out at the full moon. "I had a weird conversation with my mother today."

"What happened?"

"We were talking, and she began apologizing to me about when I had to leave college and go home to run the family business after my father's heart attack."

"It sounds like she still feels bad that you had to leave college. Did you tell her you're taking online classes?" he asked.

"Yes, but then she started talking about how my father wouldn't mind..." Her voice trailed off.

"What?"

"Oh, George." She turned to him. "Isn't it terrible that our careers keep us apart? I know you told me you'd leave the band and live at the North Pole with me, but I could never let you give up your music."

"And I wouldn't want you to give up running the family business," he said. "I know how important it is to you, and it's much more important than my job."

"I'm so glad to hear you say that." Tina breathed a sigh of relief.

"You know I support you, and I think it's kind of cool. No pun intended." He laughed and she laughed too.

"Anybody can play music, but there's only one Santa," George continued. "So, what were you saying about your conversation with your mother?"

"Oh." Tina bit her lip. "I guess technically there are two of us, and I think my father wants his job back."

***

Nick had picked up food from Isabella's favorite takeout place on his way over. It was some kind of rice and veggies with a savory sauce. The enticing aroma of garlic had filled his car.

"That smells so good."

Isabella took the bag from him when she opened the door. Her dark hair was pulled into a loose braid down her back and she wore baggy yoga pants and a top that slipped off one shoulder. She was barefoot as usual, and he took off his shoes and followed her into the living room. He became mesmerized by her braid, swinging back and forth like a pendulum as she moved.

"I'm so hungry." She sat cross-legged on the floor and dug into the cartons of food that she'd taken out of the bag and set on the coffee table.

"Robin gave me the tour schedule," he said, sitting on the couch.

Robin was their mutual manager. He had gotten *Black Ice* the coveted gig of opening for *Rock Goddess* on tour. Despite the difference in their shows, it had been an immense success, and Nick had become enamored with Isabella.

"I just got it too, but let's not talk about business tonight." She handed him a plate and watched as he spooned rice onto it.

"Thanks for picking up the food, Nicky. I love it when you do my bidding." She giggled as he scowled. "You still like me, don't you? Because I like you."

Isabella gazed at him with those clear blue (or were they green?) eyes that seemed to look right into his soul.

"Right." Nick looked down at his plate. Sometimes his mind went blank around her. Sometimes it just went blank, anyway.

"It's yummy, isn't it? I wish it was organic. I hate supporting the chemical companies, and I buy only organic at the grocery store," Isabella said.

"The big corporations are poisoning the environment," he intoned. "They're the ones who really rule the world. They buy the politicians who become their puppets."

"Uh huh." She scooped more veggies onto her plate.

"We live in a corporatocracy that's ruining the planet..."

"I recycle and use my own shopping bags," she said. "We all have to do our part."

"Right. Well, they're disrespecting nature, man, by dumping all their dirty waste into the water and air. We're being slowly poisoned."

"Let me get us some water. I have a filter in the kitchen." She jumped up and went into the kitchen. "Go on," she said when she returned, placing two glasses on the table.

"Uh." Nick struggled to regain his thoughts. "It's affecting the weather. Floods, droughts, fires..."

"And brimstone." She giggled. "Sorry. You know I totally agree with you."

"We need a revolution. The masses have to rise up..."

"I don't believe in violence."

"We need a revolution," Nick repeated. "It's the only way to change things..."

"I love it when you get intense." Isabella had a little smile on her face. Was she not taking him seriously?

"Uh..." His mind went blank again.

"I totally get what you're saying. One of the things I like about you is that you're so passionate about justice." A forkful of food was poised in front of her mouth. A mushroom fell back onto her plate. "But let's not talk about that stuff tonight."

"Right." Nick focused on eating, and they were silent for a few minutes.

"Do you remember those movies I told you about?" Isabella pointed her fork at him. "I really wanted to share some of them with you. As an artist and musician, I think you'll appreciate these classics." She picked up a DVD from the table. "The songs in these musicals convey what the characters are feeling. It pulls you into the mood and the choreography just adds to the whole..."

"Musicals?" he said with disdain.

"Nicky, give them a chance and you'll see what I mean. These songs nail it at telling stories and creating a mood, and aren't we just storytellers?"

Nick reflected on this. "My songs have messages. It's important to wake up the masses."

"Okay. You have a different goal when you write than I do. I try to weave a story and a certain mood." Isabella sighed. "I know deep down you're really a sensitive guy. We express ourselves through our music."

"Right." Nick frowned. "But musicals aren't my thing."

Isabella stood and put her hand on her hip. "I thought you agreed to watch some of these movies with me. These movies are the foundation of my love for music."

"Right."

It was going to be a long, boring night.

***

Tina opened her laptop on the dining room table. She could smell Gemma's coffee as she stared at her own screen.

"Pancakes?" George set down glasses of orange juice for them.

"Yes, please!" Gemma said.

"That sounds good," Tina concurred.

"I love it that my brothers cook," Gemma said and looked back at her computer screen.

Tina was happy to see an email from Lisa. She missed her friend.

Tina,

Hello from paradise. It's just too perfect here. It makes me nervous, although they do have big scary bugs. There are all kinds of cute little animals too, but you have to watch out for the monkeys. They're kleptomaniacs. Walter chased one of them all over when he snatched my sunglasses off a table. It was pretty funny and so sweet of him to rescue my glasses when the monkey dropped them.

Anyway, now Walter wants to buy a place here. I know he's been saying this all along, but we're actually looking at places, which is a whole other level of reality. I'm still getting used to living together, but now I'm freaking out because what happens if he actually retires and we move here? I can't live here every day. How would you and I get into trouble? You see my point?

Walter is bugging me to go to dinner, so I have to go. See you soon.

Your bestie,
Lisa

Lisa always put a smile on Tina's face. She didn't like the thought of so much distance between them, either. All her problems seemed to involve distance somehow. Either she was too far from George or too far from Lisa. She could hear George in the kitchen and a wonderful smell drifted out. She typed.

Hi Lisa,

So good to hear from you! I miss you. I would hate it if you were gone all the time, but I know Walter really wants to retire there. Hopefully, it won't happen for a while and then you'll just have to visit us or we'll visit you.

Gemma is here now, and we told her who I am and she didn't believe us! That was a surprise. I don't know how to convince her.

Then, I had a weird conversation with my mother. I think my father wants his job back because he's bored. Why didn't I see this coming? Just when I thought everything was finally running smoothly.

Say Hi to Walter.

Tina

She got up and went into the kitchen to help George.

"What can I do?" she asked.

"Just take that plate out to Gemma." He pointed with his spatula. "Oh, and grab the maple syrup."

Tina felt bad about their conversation the night before. Perhaps she shouldn't have mentioned that her father wanted his job back. She might be jumping to conclusions and there was nothing to it. She probably should've just kept her mouth shut. Now he knew that, unlike him, she wasn't willing to give up her career to be together. Why had she opened her big mouth?

George hadn't said much, and she was afraid it might be bothering him, but he might not have seen it that way. Of course! He must know that she truly loved him with all her heart and that she had an obligation to carry out the tradition of her family. Surely he understood that and would never expect her to choose.

Besides, he was a musician and could be replaced in the band. But she couldn't be replaced. Except, apparently, she could be replaced by her father now. That was the twist that altered this quandary. If it were true. Still, she hadn't let George consider the option when he'd mentioned leaving the band, so she hoped he'd extend the same courtesy and support her in doing what she loved. She wished Gemma wasn't there, so she could reassure him. She felt she had failed the night before.

"George makes the best pancakes," Gemma commented. "Don't tell Garrett I said that."

"He's a chef. He's a much better cook than me." George carried two plates to the table and set one before Tina.

"How was your date with Loren?" Tina asked.

"It was nice. We got something to eat and just hung out. He talked about the band a lot."

"Yeah?" George took a sip of Tina's orange juice.

"He really loves being in the band and he has no aspirations to take it over like Nick thinks."

"I think they're over that." George poured maple syrup over his pancakes.

"There's still a little rivalry," Gemma said.

"Nick and George were the ones who started the band." Tina defended her brother.

"Yeah. He's just happy to be a part of it."

"So, you really like him," Tina noted.

"Yeah. I do." A smile tugged at Gemma's lips.

"Just be careful," George warned.

"Don't worry about me. I can handle myself," Gemma said. "We've spent a lot of time together, and I think I know him pretty well by now."

"I've known him a lot longer and I've seen how he can be with women," George said.

Gemma made a face. "Whatever. We're just having fun."

"Are you going to see him today?" Tina asked hopefully. It would give her a chance to talk to George.

"We're going to the beach. Want to come?"

"Sounds fun," George answered.

"Oh," Tina said involuntarily. They both turned to her. "It's just... I can't spend too much time in the sun. I get sunburned."

"You've gotten some color since you've been here," George observed. "We just won't stay too long. You could use some vitamin D before you head up north."

"To the North Pole, right?" Gemma covered her mouth with a napkin as she laughed.

5 *Lotion Motion*

Clara and Santa strolled along the boardwalk. There was a cool breeze coming off the Atlantic Ocean, and it almost blew her straw hat off. She pushed it back down on her head and peered at Santa through her sunglasses. He was wearing his *Black Ice* baseball cap.

"So…" She wasn't sure how to bring up the subject. "I'm glad we got out of the condo. It's a nice day."

"Hmm." Sometimes he was a man of few words.

"So…" she said again.

"What is it?" he asked impatiently.

"I was just thinking how lucky we are. We have two wonderful children. Our son is a successful musician doing what he loves, and our daughter is running the company."

"Yes, I suppose it all worked out for the best."

"The only problem is…"

"I miss it."

Clara stopped walking. She was surprised he'd said it out loud. "I knew it!"

"Keep walking so we can get this over with."

"We're strolling, dear. We're not supposed to hurry and get it over with. We're supposed to enjoy walking. That's what strolling is." She took his hand, and they continued on.

"I'm not saying I want to go back," Santa emphasized. "I just miss it, that's all."

"I made you retire too early after your heart attack." Clara shook her head at herself.

"I'm not saying that."

"I know, but I was thinking about how unfair it was to make Tina leave college. She didn't have time to finish and she never will if we make her stay up there."

"She doesn't need to finish. She has a job."

Clara stopped and watched some seagulls strutting on the sand. A few sailed overhead, cawing.

"Tina and George haven't had much time together

since they got married last year."

Santa looked at her suspiciously. "What are you getting at, Clara?"

"Nothing. We're just having a conversation."

"Hmm." He resumed walking. "If Nick had taken over in the first place like he was supposed to, we wouldn't be in this mess."

"We're not in a mess, dear," she said. "We would've been in a mess if your brother's son had taken over."

He nodded. "Kris is incompetent."

"I don't know what your brother was thinking."

"He thought he was really going to run the family business. He always wanted to get his hands on it," Santa said.

"He seems to be okay with Tina in charge, especially since he read the history that revealed that it was supposed to be a woman in the first place," Clara said. "Ironic, huh?"

Santa pulled her toward a vendor. "I'm hungry. Let's get a hot dog."

Clara pulled back. "No hot dogs. We have to eat healthily. Remember what the doctor said. Diet and exercise."

"All the time?" he moaned.

"Don't you dare complain. I see you wolfing down your dinner every night."

"I don't wolf anything."

"Well, you certainly seem to enjoy a healthy diet and it agrees with you." Clara patted his tummy. "Look how much weight you've lost."

"Okay, so you make all that weird food taste good. But a little hot dog never hurt anyone." He wriggled his eyebrows at her.

Clara couldn't help laughing. "You're such a nut." She shook her head. "But the answer is still no. We'll have a snack when we get home."

***

"Isabella made me watch a musical," Nick griped to Kris as he opened a pack of sugar for his coffee. He kept his sunglasses on. It was bright, even in the diner.

"You mean like a play?" Kris spun a spoon on the table while they waited for their food.

"No. It was an old movie. Isabella is into these old musicals."

"Why?" Kris grimaced.

"She says it's where she got her love of music, but I don't get it." Nick shook his head.

"Me neither."

"The story was lit, though," Nick acknowledged. "It was about these two gangs."

"Sick."

"But they kept dancing and singing. People don't do that in real life. I like to keep it real."

"What happened to the gangs?" Kris yawned.

"One of the guys fell in love with the sister of the leader in the other gang."

"Then what happened?"

"Then they kept singing and dancing about it." Nick shook his head again.

"At least that's over with, dude."

"Not. She wants me to watch more old movies with her." Nick sipped his coffee.

How many would she expect him to watch? There couldn't be that many.

"Girls are crazy," Kris declared.

"They make no sense."

"Did she talk about Lilliana? Did she ask about me?" Kris looked up hopefully.

"It didn't come up."

"Do you think Lilliana would make me watch musicals?" Kris wondered.

"I don't know."

"Why don't they just watch them together?" Kris asked.

"Right." Nick nodded. That was a better idea.

Kris's spoon clattered onto the floor. He bent to pick

it up.

"Don't use that. Set it aside."

Kris put it on the table next to the window. "We should double-date."

"It was a really long movie," Nick complained. "I thought it would never end. Why are musicals so long?"

"What did you do after?" Kris asked.

"Nothing. She made me leave because I fell asleep a few times. Just for a minute. I don't think I missed anything." He shrugged.

Kris snickered. "You made her mad."

"I don't get these obstacles she's putting up between us. What does she care if I watch her stupid musicals or not?"

"Just tell her you're not watching any more of them," Kris advised. "That's what I'd do."

Easy for him to say, Nick thought.

"We should double date," Kris said again.

***

"Let me do your back."

George stood over Tina, holding the bottle of suntan lotion. She couldn't see his eyes through his sunglasses.

"I don't want to lie down yet."

Tina was watching Gemma and Loren frolic in the ocean. Everything seemed easy for them. Things weren't serious yet.

"I can do it while you're sitting up. Did you do your arms and legs?" George asked.

"Yes." She smiled up at him.

He squatted behind her and massaged the cool lotion into her skin. His warm hands felt nice. Once finished, he plopped down beside her on the plaid blanket and began busily smoothing suntan lotion onto his arm and shoulder.

"Mmm. I love that smell. It makes me think of Piña Coladas," she said.

"We can get some later."

"Okay. That sounds good."

Gemma and Loren were still in the water. Now was her chance to talk to George, but it was such a nice relaxing day that she didn't want to ruin it with a serious conversation.

"The sun feels so good." She tilted her face upward and closed her eyes.

Sand had gotten on the blanket, and she could feel the grittiness under her heels. George busily rubbed lotion onto his legs.

"Are you angry with me?" The words tumbled unexpectedly out of her mouth.

"Angry?" He looked at her with surprise. "Why would I be angry with you?"

"Because I didn't... My father could..." Tina tried to gather her thoughts. "Because I didn't take my father's offer..."

"He actually offered to take over for a few years and you turned him down?" George put the cap back on the bottle of lotion and tucked it into their beach bag.

"He didn't actually offer. My mother just brought up the idea on the phone," Tina answered. "But I let her know I wasn't interested."

George stared out at the rolling waves. "I'm disappointed that you wouldn't want to take the opportunity to spend more time together."

Tina looked down at the sand. She felt terribly guilty. "I'm afraid of losing the momentum I've built up at the company. Things are going in such a good direction. My father might undo..."

"I know," he said abruptly. He really was a bit upset with her.

"Please try to understand," she implored.

"I do." He continued staring straight ahead. "I was willing to leave the band for you, but you're not willing to make the same sacrifice for me."

"But it's not the same," Tina reasoned.

How could she make George truly understand? She

felt drops of cold water on her legs.

"The water's great," Loren enthused.

He dried himself with a towel while Gemma shook out their blanket, which scattered sand onto theirs.

"Oops. Sorry," she said. She squeezed water out of her soggy ponytail. "It's a little cold, but once you get in, it's great."

Tina squinted up at them. George reached into the beach bag and retrieved her sunglasses.

"Why aren't you wearing your sunglasses? You know how sensitive your eyes are," he admonished.

"Thanks." Tina took them and put them on.

"Hey," George murmured. "I still love you." He gave her a quick kiss.

6 *Tummy Twist*

"Hey, what was it like working for Santa?" Lisa poked Walter as they lounged in their cottage.

Walter lowered his book. "Haven't you asked me that before?"

"I know, but you never told me much, and I'm bored." She picked up a magazine.

"We can't be doing something every minute. I just want to relax and read for a bit." He uncrossed his legs on the ottoman.

Lisa went over to the bed and sat cross-legged on the floral bedspread.

"Read out loud to me."

"I can't. I'm in the middle of the book. I don't want to start over."

She yawned as she flipped through a magazine.

"Take a nap if you're tired," he suggested.

"I can't take naps. If I fall asleep, I'll be out for hours."

Walter tried to focus on his book again. "Why are you asking about working for Santa?"

"I was just wondering what it'll be like."

"Why would you say that?" He wrinkled his brow.

"Tina emailed saying that Santa wants his job back," Lisa said nonchalantly. "I might have to move my desk into your office. I don't think he'll want me sharing his."

"Wait a minute." Walter set his book down. "Are you sure about this? What's Tina going to do?"

Lisa shrugged. "Probably go back to college."

"That can't be right. What did she say?"

"She said he wants his job back because he's bored. That's no surprise. You can only play so much golf."

"Are you sure about this?" Walter got up and paced. "Let me see the email."

Lisa untangled her legs and retrieved her laptop, setting it on the little table in their room and logging on.

"Do you think he'll change anything?" she asked.

"I hope not." Walter came over and scanned her emails over her shoulder. "Let's not jump to conclusions."

"Is he really a grumpy boss? You always said he was really grumpy."

"It's a high-stress job and got to be too much. That's why he retired." Walter rubbed his clean-shaven chin. "I can't imagine that he'd want to come back after all this time."

"I wonder if he'll fire me. He might not want an assistant." Lisa looked at Walter with alarm.

"I'm sure you didn't read Tina's email right," Walter assured her. "She would've contacted me if something like this was going on."

Lisa opened the email, and Walter skimmed it.

"It doesn't sound like the decision has been made yet," he said with relief.

"I don't know," Lisa said doubtfully. "He's the big boss. If he wants his job back..."

"Tina's the boss now."

"She doesn't sound too happy, so something must be going on," Lisa surmised. "There can't be two bosses."

"Tina's the boss," Walter asserted. "Remember when Clara and Santa kept insisting that Nick was going to take over?"

"That was never going to happen."

"Exactly. And then her Uncle Kris tried to get her to hand it over to her cousin." Walter began to pace again. "She had to fight to keep control."

"But she never had to fight her own father for it," Lisa pointed out. "The real Santa."

"She's the real Santa now," Walter said adamantly. "It was always supposed to be a woman, anyway, according to the history."

"Tina would never defy her parents," Lisa said.

Walter stopped and turned to her. "You're right. She'll do whatever they want."

"We're doomed," Lisa said dramatically.

"It doesn't look definite yet," he said optimistically. "Email Tina and ask her what's going on. We need to know."

"Okay."

"Why didn't you tell me any of this before?"

"I didn't really think much about it. I was distracted by other issues."

"What other issues?"

"Our... plans. You know, deciding where to live and stuff."

Walter looked over her shoulder again. "Did they tell Gemma? Why would they do that? I don't understand what's going on."

"I know. We go on vacation for a few months and all hell breaks loose." Lisa furrowed her brow as she typed.

Walter and I are totally freaking out. Is your father taking over right away? Do I have to vacate your office? Why are you letting this happen? Why didn't you consult your best friend? Why are you blabbing to Gemma? I know she's your sister-in-law, but you better not replace me!

I guess I can't complain. It's been a good few years. But I'm not ready to retire! In Costa Rica. Far away from civilization. It's always something. Except that I don't know what this something is. Walter is bugging me to send this email. I wish my phone worked. Will your father fire me? I haven't run out of my 20 questions yet. I'll think of more.

***

Tina read the first email. Why was this getting out of hand just because of a conversation with her mother? She opened Lisa's second email.

Where am I going to go when Walter and I have a fight? Is this because you want to go back to school and you miss your perfect husband? I don't know why I'm freaking out. I actually get along great with your father. I still want to know what's happening. Where are you? Why haven't you answered my email yet?

"What are you doing? I think we should talk."

George came out of the bedroom. His hair was damp from his shower.

"I think I'm a little sunburned," Tina said.

"Where? You don't look sunburned."

"The backs of my knees and my toes," she responded. "Maybe a little on my neck, but it's not bad."

"Good. We were pretty careful."

"Yes. I just want to send a quick email to Lisa. Where's Gemma? Is she in the guest room?"

"She left with Loren while you were in the shower. I'm glad we have a little privacy."

Tina smiled nervously. She wasn't sure what he wanted to talk about.

"I'll be in the living room," he said. "I'm going to check out the news."

"Okay. I'll be right there."

Hi Lisa,

There's no reason to freak out. Nothing's going on. My mother just said on the phone that she thought my father might be bored. There hasn't been a serious discussion about my father coming back. I wish I'd never mentioned it, especially to George. Now I feel guilty that I don't want to take this potential opportunity to spend more time with him. Is that bad? I think I hurt his feelings. I wish you were here to talk to.

We only told Gemma because she wants to visit us up north and she doesn't believe us, anyway. I have to learn to keep my mouth shut.

Tina

She closed her laptop, took a deep breath, and went into the living room. She settled beside George on the couch. She loved the way she sank into the cushions when she sat down. It was so comfortable.

"What's on the news?" She turned her attention to the TV.

"Nothing good." George picked up the remote and turned it off.

Tina felt tiny knots twisting in her stomach. "Are you still mad at me?"

"Stop saying that, Tina. I'm not mad. Okay?"

"Okay," she said softly.

"I was thinking while I was in the shower," he said. "This might be a good chance for you to take a break from work."

"I don't need a break."

"You probably don't realize how stressful your job is. Look what happened to your father."

"That was over decades. Really. I'm fine."

"I know, but I thought you could go back to school. You gave up finishing your education to help your family, which is admirable, but now you have the chance to finish college and your job will be right there waiting for you when you're ready to go back," George rationalized.

"I'm taking online classes. I don't need to be here to finish college."

"It's not the same as attending classes." George shook his head. "Maybe I'm being selfish, but it would also give us some time together. Wouldn't it be great to be together for a while without our next separation always hanging over our heads?"

"I'd love to be with you all the time, George," Tina said fervently. "But I don't know if my father really wants to go back to work. It's just something my mother said. I don't even think she discussed it with him."

"She brought it up so she must know how he feels about it."

"Maybe. But I've also changed the way we do things."

"He knows that. Your parents were up there last season, and they were okay with everything."

"Yes, but if he were there for a while, he might start changing things back. You know we had disagreements about how to do things," Tina reminded him.

George noticed her hand on her tummy. "Is your stomach bothering you again?"

"A little," she admitted.

He shook his head in frustration. "Tina, you need this break."

"I'm not stressed about work. I love my job. It's just that everybody is putting too much pressure on me."

George stared at her for a moment. "I thought you loved *me*."

"Of course I do. I love you *and* I love my job. There's nothing wrong with that. You love your job too. Don't make me feel guilty about it."

"I'm not making you feel anything."

George shook his head and got up from the couch and walked out of the room.

Tina stared after him. They'd never had an argument before, and she wasn't sure what to do. It was the worst feeling in the world. How could George doubt her feelings for him? They had so little time together. She didn't want to spend it arguing. Why couldn't she make him understand?

7 *Pizza & Movie Night*

"You guys are quiet this morning," Gemma noticed.

"What did you and Loren do last night?" Tina asked to change the subject.

They sat in their usual spots at the dining room table, each lost in thought.

Gemma took a sip of coffee and smiled. "We got dinner and walked along the beach at night and just talked. It was so beautiful. The moon was shimmering on the water and you could hear the waves."

"Sounds nice." Tina avoided looking at George.

"We're going out dancing tonight. You guys should come," Gemma said. "Loren was telling me about this new club. It'll be so much fun. The more the merrier."

George set their orange juice on the table. "Yeah. Maybe."

"No, really. I'm only going to be here a few more nights, so you *have* to go with us. It'll be fun."

"You really like him," Tina noted.

"Yeah. Why not? I'm not taking it seriously. We live too far apart." Gemma glanced between them. "Even though it worked out for you guys. I just don't want to deal with it."

"It makes things more difficult," George said. "Both of you have to be dedicated to making it work."

Tina looked up at him, but he was facing Gemma.

"Exactly," Gemma said. "And I'm not about to move to Florida and Loren isn't going to move to Boston, so what's the point of pursuing a serious thing?"

"If you really like him, you shouldn't give up." Tina stole a glance at George. "You should be flexible. You can live here part of the year and up in Boston for the rest of the year. You could make it work."

"Of course, you want to spend as much time together as possible when you have the chance," George said, taking a sip of juice.

"What's really important is to support each other's

careers," Tina said. "You don't want to give up what you love."

"When I write, I need solitude to focus, so it's good to be alone." Gemma stirred her coffee. "But I like to take a break between books. You know, clear my head before I start another one."

"Breaks from work are good," George said.

"I always take a long break between seasons," Tina told Gemma. "It totally regenerates me and then I go back fresh and ready to work."

"Building a strong foundation for a relationship takes time," George said. "You have to be willing to spend the time to make things work."

"Yeah. That's why I'm keeping this simple," Gemma said.

"It's good to know what you're getting into." Tina's eyes met George's.

"That's why I'm keeping it casual with Loren. I have my eyes open." Gemma checked her phone. "Did I tell you I was seeing an English professor for a while?"

"No," George answered.

"He called my books trivial." Gemma frowned. "I know they're not great literature, but come on. People enjoy my books."

"And you enjoy writing them," Tina said. "That's what counts. You enjoy your job."

"Yup." Gemma took a sip of coffee.

George got up and came over to Tina. She looked up at him and he leaned down to give her a kiss.

"Aw, that's sweet," Gemma said. "I'm hungry. What's for breakfast?"

"Coming up," George said, not taking his eyes off Tina. "How about a breakfast burrito?"

"That sounds perfect," Tina said as a feeling of relief flooded her.

***

"Hey, George." Loren sidled up to him at rehearsal, adjusting his guitar over his shoulder and kicking aside a mass of wires strewn across the floor.

"Hey, Loren." George was searching for his favorite pick in his guitar case.

"It's stuffy in here," John complained.

"It's a basement. Don't be an ingrate," Milo said.

"Don't you have a fan or something?" John asked.

"I have one upstairs. I'll go get it." Milo set down his drumsticks and went upstairs, each wooden stair creaking.

"You know, since I joined the band, we've hardly hung out together," Loren pointed out. "We used to hang out all the time in our other band."

"We were younger then." George shrugged.

"And now you're married and too busy for your friends," Loren teased.

"Well, that..."

"I'm just kidding." Loren nudged him. "But now I'm seeing your sister. I hope that doesn't bother you."

"Kind of late for that," John commented.

"Not a problem," George said. "Gemma can make her own decisions. Besides, it's not serious."

"Who said it's not serious?" Loren asked.

"Anybody want something to drink?" John asked, heading upstairs.

"Water," Loren called after him. "So, Nick. What are you doing after rehearsal?"

"Huh?" Nick looked up from his notebook. He was still trying to determine the best song sequence for their tour.

"He's got a hot date with Isabella," Kris piped up, clutching a tangle of wires he couldn't seem to untangle and throwing them down.

"Yeah?" Loren grinned at Nick. "Awesome."

"If she doesn't make me watch another musical," Nick grumbled.

"Sometimes I like musicals," George said.

"Are you and Tina going out with us tonight?" Loren

asked. "Gemma's only going to be around for a few more nights."

"Okay. Sure," George answered.

"I don't know how you do it, man." Loren shook his head. "It's got to suck when Tina's gone."

"It does," George affirmed. He'd found his pick and held it in his teeth while he tuned his guitar.

"It's not like you can just run up to the North Pole all the time," Loren remarked.

The pick fell out of George's mouth. "What?"

Nick looked up again. "Huh?"

"I thought it was a secret," Kris said, furrowing his brow.

Loren started chuckling. "Gemma told me what you told her. Like she was going to believe it. Pretty twisted."

George and Nick exchanged looks.

"Right." Nick turned his attention back to his notebook.

"Yeah. Funny," George said.

"What's funny?" Kris asked.

"I found a fan," Milo announced, descending the stairs with a small fan followed by John.

"Courtney doesn't want me drinking beer this early," John was saying.

"You married guys are whipped." Milo set the fan in a corner and plugged it in. "Loren, promise me you won't cave, man."

"It's too late," Kris taunted. "Just you and me are free and single, Milo."

"Sad." Milo shook his head.

"North Pole." Loren chuckled softly.

"What are you talking about?" Milo picked up his drumsticks.

"Nothing. Inside joke," George blurted. "Nick, what song are we starting with?"

"Huh?" Nick looked up.

"'Frost in My Head'? 'Sucked into the Machine'? What do you think, Loren?" George asked, hoping to distract him.

"There are no secrets between bandmates," John warned.

Loren glanced up. "Oh, Tina told Gemma…"

"Come on," Milo groaned loudly. "We're not interested in your women. This is a wife and girlfriend-free zone."

"Milo's right," George said quickly. "Let's rehearse."

"And no girls either," Kris said. "No girls or women or wives or girlfriends. Just us guys."

***

Isabella flung open the door. With a little smile, she took the pizza from Nick and silently turned toward the living room. He stepped inside and followed her.

She spun and pointed to his feet. "Shoes."

He pushed the door closed and removed his shoes.

"I hardly ever eat pizza," she confessed, setting the box down on the coffee table. "But I had a craving."

She wore a loose, floral, sleeveless dress. Her hair hung in two long braids and her lips were shiny with lip gloss. A candle was burning and the sweet scent of vanilla lingered in the air until she opened the pizza box. She kneeled and handed Nick a plate.

"Music?" he asked, hoping for a movie-less evening.

"Mmm." She took a large bite out of a slice of pizza and wiped her mouth with a napkin. While chewing, she handed him a DVD.

"Another musical?" He didn't bother to hide his disappointment.

"Nicky, I told you we were going to watch my musicals," Isabella said. "This one is shorter, but you're going to love it."

It didn't seem like she had any idea about what he loved. Or maybe she did, and that's why she knew he'd put up with her stupid musicals.

"Okay, so this one is about a con man who goes from town to town, but then he falls in love with the librarian and it complicates his plans." She put her hand over her mouth. "Oh, I'm giving too much away."

"Right. Just put it on and let's get this over with." Nick picked up a slice of pizza.

"Don't be like that." Isabella stood and put her hand on her hip. Her curvaceous hip. She smiled playfully and ran her fingers down his cheek. He froze mid-chew.

"Now, Nicky, I want to share myself with you," she murmured. "I want us to connect on a deeper level. Don't you want that with me? Maybe I should call Loren and see if he wants to come over."

"He's with Gemma."

It gave Nick great satisfaction to say that. She could no longer use Loren to make him jealous.

"Gemma?" She stood up.

"George's sister." He picked up the DVD from the coffee table. "Put it on. I want to see what happens with the con man and the librarian."

A smile lit up her face. "You're going to love this movie."

"How many more musicals do you have, anyway?" He tried to sound casual.

"Um, probably about twenty or so." Isabella laughed suddenly. "You should see the look on your face. I'm just messing with you."

He scowled.

"Really, Nicky. You're an artist. You should appreciate this. Do you ever watch music videos?"

"Nah. Music is music."

"Robin's been talking to me about doing a music video," Isabella said thoughtfully.

"No way I'm doing a music video," he vowed.

"He's a good manager. He knows what we need to do to stay on top. It's a competitive business," she said. "Anyway, I think it would be fun. *Rock Goddess* could do an amazing video. We could make it dreamy and magical with drifting fog."

"*Black Ice* is never doing a music video," Nick said decisively. "It wouldn't be right for our type of music."

"What if he wants us to do one of our duets?" she

asked. "You know the fans love it when we sing together on tour."

Nick shook his head. "My music is a spontaneous experience."

"I know." She slid next to him on the couch. "This is what I like about you. You're unpredictable and passionate."

She put her finger under his chin and gave him a sweet kiss. What was that taste? Nick's mind went totally blank.

Isabella jumped up. "Now for the movie. I can't wait for you to see it!"

8 *Pink Glitter*

"Are you going to retire if Santa takes over?" Lisa asked Walter in a low voice.

"It doesn't sound like we need to worry about it." He picked up his menu.

They were sitting at an outdoor table. The fabric of the umbrella shading them fluttered in the gentle breeze. It was another leisurely day.

"But what if he does? Don't you think Tina would jump at the chance to spend more time with George?"

"I don't think she will," he said slowly.

"Why not? Don't you think she wants to spend more time with her husband?" Lisa frowned. "Tina is too perfect and her life is too perfect. Don't you hate them?"

"No. How can you say that? You're her best friend."

"Fine. I don't really hate her. Don't take me so literally. Where's my drink?" Lisa looked around for the server. "What were we talking about?"

"I said I don't think that Tina would let her father take over the business. She's put too much into it and she wouldn't want to risk him undoing all the progress she's made."

"That's true." She put down her menu. "What if she does, though? Will you stay? What if he fires me? Would you still stay?"

"Let's not cross that bridge until we come to it, okay?" Walter glanced around. "Where are our drinks?"

The server approached, balancing a tray. "Here you go. Sorry about the wait. Are you ready to order?"

They gave her their orders, and each took a long sip of their sweet tropical drink.

"Not quite as good as the Polar Coladas at the Snowed Inn & Pub," Lisa commented. "But pretty darn yummy."

"Or the Borealis Blizzards at the Northern Lights Festival," Walter added.

"Those are so good, but you can only drink one."

"Only half of one."

Lisa sighed. "Life has been such an adventure since I moved up to the North Pole."

"Keep your voice down," Walter cautioned.

"Do you remember the first time we met?"

"I'll never forget it. The first time I saw you, you and Tina were drunk."

Lisa giggled.

"I'd never seen Tina like that, and I didn't know who the heck you were. We never had visitors."

"I was in a daze. I couldn't believe everything I was seeing. Who knew the North Pole actually exists?" she said in a hushed tone. "It blew my mind. You grew up there and you're used to it, but for someone like me..." She took another long sip of her drink. "It's funny that even after that interview Tina did last year, people still don't believe."

"That's a good thing," Walter said. "I know Tina had good intentions, but it's better this way. I don't know why they told Gemma."

"Tina's email said they told her because she wants to visit them up north. But it doesn't matter because she didn't believe them."

"Would you?"

"Probably not."

A breeze lifted Lisa's paper napkin and dropped it by her feet. She bent to retrieve it and placed it under her glass.

"Oh, Walter. It's so peaceful here. I understand why you like it so much." Lisa took a deep breath. "Buy that place if you want to. I'll live anywhere with you."

"Do you mean that?" He took her hand. "I'd rather be here. It's too crowded in Florida."

"You're right."

"And they have hurricanes."

"Oh, my gosh. I forgot about that."

"I warned Clara and Santa before they bought the condo years ago." Walter shook his head. "And now the storms have only gotten worse. They've been lucky so far."

"Wow. What about here? Do they have hurricanes here?" she wondered.

"It's too far south, but they can get heavy rain," Walter said. "Really intense rainstorms and flooding. I researched it before I decided to buy property here."

"You're so practical," Lisa said with admiration. "See? I wouldn't have even thought of doing that."

***

"I'm so pale," Tina complained, studying herself in the bathroom mirror.

"Are you kidding? You look incredible."

Gemma fluffed her thick hair and leaned into the mirror to check her face.

Tina brushed her hair. "My hair is flat and I have no color in my face."

Gemma shook her head. "Let me French braid your hair. Then just put on a little mascara and some eyeshadow and you'll look phenomenal."

"You think so?"

"Yeah. You have classic beauty. Not like me. I look more bohemian." Gemma shrugged. "I can't pull off classy and sophisticated like you can."

Tina waved her hand. "I don't have the confidence for that."

"Or maybe you're not snobby enough." Gemma laughed. "I'm glad you guys are going out with us tonight."

"Me too." Tina brushed mascara on her eyelashes. It felt like she was playing dress-up. "I hardly ever wear makeup."

"You don't need it," Gemma said, watching her.

"Thanks."

Perhaps this was what she and George needed. A night out. Things hadn't been the same since their spat. She hated feeling like there was a barrier between them, but she couldn't seem to figure out how to get past it.

Gemma stood behind her and braided her hair. Tina had put on a black and hot pink top that George liked. She was hoping he'd find her irresistible and that their differences would melt away on the dance floor.

"Oh!" Gemma cried. "I know what would look great on you. I have pink eyeshadow with glitter in it. I never use it. It came with another one I bought, but it would look perfect on you."

"Okay."

Gemma finished braiding her hair and dug around in her makeup bag.

"Got it. Close your eyes and I'll put it on you."

Tina stood still and felt the soft brush moving across her eyelids.

"It looks good," Gemma said. "I like it."

Tina opened her eyes and turned to the mirror. Her eyes were framed with mascara and sparkled when she moved.

Gemma took her hand and pulled her out to the living room where George and Loren were waiting.

"Wow, we're lucky guys, George." Loren noticed them first.

George approached Tina and peered at her. "What did you put on your eyes?"

Gemma hit his shoulder. "Say something nice to your wife."

George smiled. "You look beautiful, but you always look beautiful."

Tina blushed.

***

They found a high round table at the trendy new club and seated themselves. The place was filling up quickly, and it was loud. They yelled their drink orders to the cocktail server. Retro disco glitter balls hung from the ceiling as people milled about. Tina hung onto George's arm. A DJ played dance music and Gemma and Loren got up to dance.

"We'll watch the table," George yelled to them.

"I guess we can't all dance together," Tina said in his ear.

He shook his head and sipped his drink. "Wow, that's strong."

Tina took a sip of hers. It felt good going down and helped to relax her.

George turned to her. "You look very pretty."

Tina smiled and looked down at the table. Her eyes fell on her ring. The blue stone and Swarovski crystals glistened. Love for George filled her. She was so lucky. She took a big gulp of her drink and bobbed her head to the beat, searching for Gemma and Loren on the dance floor, but she couldn't find them in the crowd.

They finally returned to the table, breathless. Gemma fanned herself with her hand while Loren chugged his beer. A slower song was beginning, and Tina grabbed George's hand.

"Our turn!"

She pulled him onto the dance floor and wrapped her arms around him. It felt so good to be in his embrace.

"I miss you so much when we're apart," she said in his ear.

He held her tighter. "I miss you too."

Tina closed her eyes and rested her head on his shoulder while they swayed together silently, making her a little dizzy. Then, abruptly, the pounding beat returned, and they danced amidst the jostling throng. Tina let the beat move her and it felt freeing. She was glad they were out dancing instead of sitting at home being gloomy with each other. Why did things have to be so serious? She wished Lisa were here. They always had so much fun together. They were young and life was good. She had a fabulous best friend and the best husband ever. Just why couldn't they all be in the same place all the time?

***

"Last night was fun," Loren said to George as he sat down on Nick's worn couch.

"What happened last night?" Kris asked.

"We double-dated," George said.

"We went to that new club downtown," Loren added. "It was lit."

"It was mobbed, and the drinks were too strong," George said and then smiled. "Yeah, it was lit."

"I should've gone," Kris said. "I bet the girls were hot."

"Courtney and I went there one night, and it was way too crowded. You could hardly move," John said. "Someone stepped on her toe so we had to leave."

"Boo hoo," Milo said.

"Hey, they almost broke her toe," John responded. "Don't be a jerk."

"How's Isabella?" George asked Nick when he came back from the kitchen carrying a six-pack.

Nick handed beers out and grimaced.

"What's wrong?" George asked, shaking his head at the beer Nick held out. He set it on the coffee table.

"He had to watch another musical," Kris shared solemnly.

George laughed. "That's not so bad. At least you get to spend time with her."

"Okay, guys." Their manager, Robin, stood before them with his hands clasped. "It's all good news."

Kris knocked his beer over on the coffee table. "Hey. You shouldn't have put your keys there," he said to George. "Look what you made me do."

Nick went into the kitchen and returned with a sponge and a roll of paper towels.

"Okay," Robin continued. "Sales are great and I think *Black Ice* is ready to headline a tour."

"Whoa! That's awesome!" Loren enthused.

Nick stopped wiping the table and handed the sponge to Kris. "But I thought we were doing another tour with *Rock Goddess*."

"That's right. You're going to hit some major cities in a few months, but then they're doing a European tour later this year. Didn't Isabella tell you?"

Everyone looked at Nick.

"It didn't come up." He sank back down into his overstuffed chair.

Kris snickered.

"But what about our duets?" Nick asked. "The fans love our duets."

"*You* love the duets." Kris snickered again.

Milo hit him on the shoulder. "Shut up."

"Hey!" Kris rubbed his shoulder.

"Yes, that's true, but we have to get you out on your own. The duets are good for single song sales and also boost album sales for CD and vinyl for both bands." Robin rubbed his hands together. "You guys are ready for your own tour, and I have a good up-and-coming band that can open for you. Then, if all goes well, we'll get you over to Europe too. This is very exciting news for the band. We're moving up to the next level. So keep churning out those songs."

Nick sat cogitating on this news. It was good for the band, but after their next tour, their professional relationship with *Rock Goddess* would end. Would Isabella find a new musician to tease in their next opening band? This was a crisis of epic proportions.

9 *Friend Zone*

"Does everybody have enough gravy?" Clara asked, hovering at the table. "Kris? Nick?"

"I want more gravy," Santa said.

"Tina? George?" Clara stood poised with the gravy boat.

"I said I want more gravy," Santa repeated.

Clara held up her hand. "I know. Let me get everyone else fixed up first. Don't worry, dear. There's plenty."

"Nick, that's great news about the band," Tina enthused.

"Did Gemma get to the airport okay?" Clara asked, seating herself at the table. "Did I forget anything?"

"I don't have a knife," Kris said.

"You don't need a knife. You can cut the veggie loaf with your fork," she said.

"Yes, Gemma got home already," George said.

"Where's the meat?" Kris asked, poking at his food.

Clara let out an exasperated sigh. "Kris, you know we don't eat meat. That's how your uncle lost weight. Doesn't he look healthier?"

Kris furrowed his brow and peered at Santa. "He looks mad."

"I'm not mad," Santa grumbled. "I just want more gravy."

"Oh, sorry, dear." Clara passed the gravy boat to him. "Now what's this news about the band, Nick?"

"We're going to headline our own tour," Nick replied without enthusiasm.

"Oh, isn't that good?" Clara asked.

"Yes. It means our sales are good and we can carry a tour on our own without another band headlining," George explained.

"It means they're the main band, Mom," Tina clarified.

"That sounds like a good thing," Clara said. "But

you don't look happy, Nick."

"He's bummed out because he won't get to see Isabella anymore." Kris nudged him.

"Why not?" Clara wondered.

"We won't be touring with her band anymore. *Rock Goddess* is going to do a European tour," George said.

"A European tour? They must be very popular," Clara commented.

"They're hot," Kris said.

"I bet that will happen to *Black Ice* pretty soon." Tina smiled at Nick.

"Pass the salt," Santa said.

Clara made a face. "Easy on the salt, dear."

"You'll still see Isabella," Tina said to her brother. "You're friends now and sometimes you write together."

"She makes him watch musicals." Kris snorted out a laugh.

"What's wrong with musicals? I love musicals," Clara stated. "Tina, remember when you had the flu, and we watched three movies in a row? Although I don't think they were musicals."

"We both fell asleep during the last movie," Tina recalled. "And then you got sick."

"Yes. That was the year we had so many people out sick. Remember that, dear?" She turned to Santa. "Didn't Gerta and Jann help us work the production line that year?"

"Who are they?" Kris asked.

"They're Kai's parents. You remember Kai," Clara said.

"Wasn't Kai your boyfriend?" Kris asked Tina.

Tina glanced at George. "He was my boyfriend in high school."

"Love sucks," Nick declared.

"That's why I'm single," Kris said, chewing.

"Is there more gravy?" Santa asked. "I don't think you made enough gravy."

"Relationships can be difficult," Clara said sympathetically.

"Just hang in there," George encouraged. "She likes you or she wouldn't want to share something she enjoys with you."

"What does she enjoy?" Kris dropped his fork in his lap.

"Musicals." Santa pounded his fist on the table and made everyone jump. "Now, is there more gravy or not?"

"It's right in the kitchen on the stove." Clara got up. "Sorry, dear."

"Dad, you could get it yourself." Tina pointed out.

"That's okay." Clara went to the kitchen and refilled the gravy boat. "Here you go, dear. Now, what were we talking about?"

"Gerta," Tina said suddenly.

"We were talking about Gerta?" Clara asked, wrinkling her brow.

"No, Mom." Tina looked at Nick. "You should come up to the Pole this year. You can go to the Northern Lights Festival and you can see Gerta."

"Why would I want to see Kai's mother?" Nick asked.

"Because she can give you good advice," she answered. "She's... psychic. She just knows things."

"Why would he want to see someone psycho?" Kris shook his head.

"Psychic, you idiot," Santa blurted.

"Dear, that's not nice." Clara patted his hand. "Gerta is really gifted."

"She's always right." Tina nodded.

"She predicts things?" George sopped up a puddle of gravy with a roll.

"Well, it's not exactly like that," Tina said. "She just knows things. She gives advice."

Tina longed for the warmth of Gerta's kitchen and her sage guidance. Yes, she would see Gerta when she returned home. She always felt grounded after her visits, and things seemed clearer. She noticed Nick was sulking. He could definitely benefit from a visit with Gerta.

***

"Home sweet home." Lisa fell back on the couch at Walter's house. "What a long flight. I just want to sleep for twelve hours."

"Let's take it easy for a few days before we go into the office," Walter suggested.

Lisa slipped down off the small couch and pushed herself back up. "I'm sorry the sale for that property fell through."

"It's probably for the best." He sat beside her. "I was thinking on the plane that I probably haven't been fair to you."

"What do you mean?" Lisa turned toward him.

Walter scanned the room. "I'm going to call a contractor and see what we can do to make the house more comfortable for you. I know it's too small."

"Or I'm too big." She giggled.

"I should probably get larger furniture too." He ran his hand along the couch cushion.

Lisa placed her hand on the worn fabric. "How about if I buy a new couch? We can pick it out together. It will be fun. Unless..."

"Unless what?"

"Unless we discover that we have totally different taste and we can't agree."

"I'm surprised when we agree on anything."

"I know. Right?"

"We have to go food shopping tomorrow. There's not much in the house," Walter said. "And we have to go out to the main barn and let the reindeer know we're back."

"Unless we see them at the pub." Lisa raised her eyebrows.

"Are you trying to tell me you want to go to the pub?"

"Why not? We could get something to eat at the Kringle Café and then get a drink or three at the pub," she said. "It'll help us unwind. My inner time clock is all discombobulated.”

“We could...”

“Ha! Unwind. Clock. Get it?” Lisa giggled again.

Walter smiled.

“Why did you say that you’re glad you didn’t get the property?” Lisa asked.

“I was thinking on the plane...”

“Why didn’t you mention it on the plane?” she wondered.

“You were asleep. Actually, you were snoring. You were really loud. It was embarrassing.”

“I was not!” Lisa shoved him and he chuckled.

“Anyway, I was thinking it might be better to buy one of those little cottages by the beach like I originally planned,” Walter said. “We don’t need a big place over there. Then we might have enough money to...”

“Buy a place in Florida, too?” Lisa shrieked.

“I was going to say travel. I don’t know whether we could afford to buy two places.”

“I have some money saved. I don’t know if it’s enough.” Lisa sank back down onto the couch. “This couch is really comfortable. I hate to make you get rid of it. You could put it in your office.”

“It might be too long.”

“We’ll measure it.”

“Okay, let’s get going. I’m hungry.”

Lisa groaned. “I hate to get all bundled up again just to go a few miles.”

“That’s life at the North Pole.” Walter shrugged.

***

“Why didn’t you tell me?” Nick demanded as soon as Isabella opened the door.

“Nice to see you, too.” She took the bag of food from him and spun around on her bare feet, causing her long braid to whip around.

Nick quickly pulled off his shoes and followed her into the living room.

"Did you lock the door?" she asked. "You know I have cray-cray fans."

"Right." He turned back to check it.

Isabella kneeled in front of the coffee table and pulled the food out of the bag.

"Which burrito is mine?"

"They're the same." He stood glaring at her.

"What? What's wrong, Nicky?" She cut her burrito in half and took a bite.

"Why didn't you tell me that this is our last tour together?" He sat down on the couch and noticed a DVD on the coffee table.

"This is a good thing for *Black Ice*." Isabella chewed.

"But... but what about our duets? The fans are into them," he said weakly.

"I am too, but this is best for our bands. It's progress."

Nick stared at her blankly. He didn't want to progress without her. He'd no longer have an excuse to see her. What if they drifted apart? Success was a double-edged blade of grass or something like that. What would he do if he couldn't see those mysterious blue or green eyes looking deep into his? What would he do if he couldn't hear her musical voice saying his name?

"Nicky."

"Huh?"

"Eat your burrito before it gets cold."

He picked it up.

"Are you afraid we won't see each other anymore?" A sly smile spread across her face. "I knew you liked me. It's always been about more than business, hasn't it?"

"Uh..." Nick wasn't sure how to answer. How could he admit that he'd had another agenda all along? How could he admit she had a hold on him? She'd backed him into a corner. Why did she have this witchy power over him?

"Oh, Nicky. I'm going to miss you too. Not just working with you, but hanging out." Isabella smiled at him, melting his insides. "But we're friends, right? We can still hang out if we want to."

"Right."

Why wasn't she aware of her true feelings for him? He had to come up with a plan to wake her up. He'd had a plan once. What was it? He took a bite of his burrito. He hadn't realized how hungry he was.

"You really get me and my music. Other guys... other musicians just want to hit on me, but you're not like that. You're truly my friend." Isabella reached over and put her hand on his hand. "I appreciate that."

Nick looked at her delicate hand resting on his. Her skin was soft and warm. Friend? How had he gotten into the friend zone? She was just messing with him. They had a powerful attraction that was apparent to everyone. People had believed they were a legit rock couple last year when they'd played it up for the press.

"We have chemistry," he stated.

She removed her hand. "That's why our duets are so powerful. And you've expanded my musical world, Nicky. We're good for each other."

They stared into each other's eyes. Maybe she was finally grasping how intertwined their souls were. Maybe she finally understood that they couldn't live without each other. The gods of rock had crossed their paths and melded their destinies... Welded? Fused? What was the right word?

"Nicky..."

"Huh?" His gaze hadn't faltered.

"I can't wait to share this movie with you." Isabella grabbed the DVD and jumped up.

"Great." Nick fell back on the couch and took another bite of his burrito. What had he just been thinking? It was something about destiny.

"This is a more recent movie. It's about a bunch of bohemians living in the city struggling with life and love and survival. You're going to love it," Isabella enthused, popping it into the DVD player.

Nick let out a deep sigh and vowed to stay awake

this time.

10 *Beatle Karma*

Tina yawned. She and George had been up late watching a movie. She knew she shouldn't sit out on the balcony too long, but the sun was warm and felt so good. George had made another big breakfast that filled her tummy and made her feel lazy. He was such a superb cook she couldn't help stuffing herself. It would be his fault if she got fat.

"Don't stay out there too long," George warned from the screen door. "You get easily sunburned."

"Come out here with me," she coaxed.

"Can't. I have stuff to do."

Tina's phone rang as she heard him walk away. It was probably her mother.

"Hello?"

"I feel like I haven't talked to you forever."

"Lisa! It's so good to hear your voice."

"Yeah. We're back. When are you coming home?"

"I'm not sure. I really wanted to stay for our first anniversary, but George will be on tour by then. It's so disappointing."

"That's a bummer," Lisa agreed.

George opened the screen door. "Who are you talking to?"

She peered up at him through her sunglasses. "Lisa."

"What?" Lisa asked.

"George wanted to know who was on the phone."

"Oh, tell him hi."

"Lisa says hi," Tina relayed.

"Hi back. I'm going to run to the store to get some veggies for dinner. Need anything?"

"Chocolate?" She smiled up at him.

"Okay. Be back in a few." He gave her a kiss.

"I totally heard that kiss. Do you know how sickening you two are?" Lisa asked.

"How was your vacation? Did you buy a place?"

"No. I've been trying to convince Walter that we should buy a place there instead, but he's really set on Costa Rica."

"Too bad. It would be fun hanging out here in Florida."

"Walter said we see each other enough as it is."

"I guess the guys would feel neglected," Tina said.

"I love Walter, but I can't talk to him like I can talk to you," Lisa admitted. "It's different."

"I know. How are you two getting along?"

"We're getting along so well, it scares me. I keep waiting for the other shoe to drop."

"There is no other shoe. Walter is a great guy. You got a good one," Tina assured her.

"I just get nervous when things go well. You know how I am."

"Yes. But you deserve to be happy. I'm glad things are good."

"Me too. How are things over there?" Lisa asked. "And by the way, why are you telling everyone who you are?"

"I'm not telling everyone. Just Gemma. She keeps saying she wants to visit us and see the toy factory, so we had to tell her, but she didn't believe us, anyway."

"Well, I know she's your sister-in-law, but don't be replacing me," Lisa warned.

Tina smiled. "I would never do that."

"Okay, bestie. How's your perfect husband? Ugh! I hate that word."

"Then just say his name." Tina shook her head. "Things are... weird. They feel off."

"What do you mean?"

"Ever since my mother brought up the possibility of my father coming back for a few seasons, George has been upset with me. I think it bothers him that I didn't jump at the chance to be here all the time with him." Tina bit her lip. "I just don't want to give up the family business. What if my father changed everything back the way it was? George just doesn't understand the position I'm in…"

"So your father *does* want to come back?"

"I don't know. I'm still planning on coming back up there, so don't worry. Nothing's changed. So far."

"Good," Lisa said with relief. "Don't scare me like that."

"I don't even want to think about work right now. I'm afraid to look at my emails." Tina closed her eyes. "Oh, the sun feels so good."

"Don't talk to me about the sun. I feel like an icicle every time I go outside," Lisa complained. "Anyway, is George still mad at you?"

"He says he's not, but it's like there's a little wedge between us now," Tina said. "I don't know what to do."

"Don't ask me. Relationships are obviously not my area of expertise."

"But you used to be a counselor."

"A school counselor," Lisa corrected. "But my best advice is just to communicate. Honestly."

"I'll try." Tina sighed.

"Oh, we ran into Kai and Sonia at the pub. He said his mother wants to see you when you get back."

"That's funny. I was just thinking about her."

"Can I go too this time?" Lisa asked. "I want to meet her. Can she read my fortune, too?"

"That's not what she does. She senses things. Maybe she can tell me what to do about George," Tina mused. "And my father. And maybe even Nick."

"What's wrong with Nick?"

"He's depressed because they're not going to open for *Rock Goddess* anymore after this tour. He's afraid he won't have an excuse to see Isabella anymore."

"Why doesn't he just tell her he likes her?"

"Exactly."

"Why aren't they going on tour together anymore?"

"Actually, it's great news," Tina said. "The band is going to headline their own tour after this one. Isn't that amazing?"

"Wow, who knew Nick would actually achieve his

dream of becoming a rock star?" Lisa said with awe. "And people don't even know who he really is."

"Can you imagine if he'd become Santa?"

"What kind of alternate reality would that be?" Lisa wondered.

"Lucky for me, he didn't want the job."

Yes, lucky indeed.

***

"I want you to talk to me, dear," Clara implored. Her legs were curled under her on the couch.

"About what?" He lowered the remote in his hand.

"Wasn't it nice having everyone over? It just doesn't seem to happen often enough. The kids are always busy with their own lives and Tina is about to head back up to the Pole." She took a deep breath. "But you wish you were the one going back, don't you?"

"I miss it sometimes."

"You'd better decide what you want to do before Tina leaves," she advised.

"I have. I'm retired." He picked up the remote. "End of story."

"I'm just tired of you moping around. I know you're bored and I know you miss it. Let's discuss this."

"I don't want my old job back," Santa grumbled. "Tina is doing a fine job."

"That's not the issue."

"What we did last year was good enough."

"You mean going up for the Northern Lights Festival and staying to help through delivery day?" Clara confirmed. "Yes, Tina sure needed our help. Things have gotten busier, haven't they?"

"The population is always growing."

"Faster than ever. At some point, we might need two Santas."

He raised his eyebrows at her. "I don't think that's an option."

Clara waved her hand at him. "No, of course not.

Tina manages the deliveries just fine."

"Why did you bring this up? Did Tina say she wants a break?" he questioned.

"No. I just started thinking about how she probably wants to finish college and spend more time with her husband. I want her to have that opportunity now that you're better. We could give that to her."

"Hmm."

"What are you thinking?" Clara asked.

"I think I'm going to watch some TV." Santa pointed the remote at the TV.

***

"Nick, you have to let the rest of us contribute more songs to our CDs," Milo demanded.

The guys were sprawled around Nick's living room for the band meeting. Beer bottles sat on the coffee table and there were two open bags of potato chips John had brought.

"Milo's right," John said. "You're really prolific, but the rest of us want our stuff recorded too."

"This is what broke up the Beatles," Nick moaned. "Everybody was against Paul."

"You're not Paul. I'm Paul," John argued.

"You're John," Nick said.

"Just because my name is John doesn't mean I'm John. I think George is John."

"George is George," Nick said adamantly.

"Who am I, then?" Milo asked. "There was no black Beatle."

"You're the fifth Beatle," Kris said. "There are five in the band now."

"There was no fifth Beatle," Milo scoffed.

"I could be the fifth Beatle," Kris offered.

"You're not even in the band." Milo shook his head.

"It's karma, man. We're just like the Beatles," Nick asserted.

"We're nothing like the Beatles," Milo said.

"We started with four band members and two of them are named John and George," Nick argued. "And George is vegetarian, and we got discovered by a manager who's making us successful."

"Our music is totally different," Milo pointed out.

"It's about the formula and karma," Nick insisted.

"Whatever." Milo waved his hand dismissively.

"I want to do another duet with Isabella for the CD," Nick said. "Those songs sell. The fans love them."

"You just want an excuse to see her," John accused. "Those songs don't really work with the rest of our stuff."

"He's right. Our stuff is edgier," Loren agreed. "I thought that was our image."

"We've had some softer stuff mixed in," George said. "My songs aren't edgy."

"That's because you're in love. See what that does to the band?" Milo shot looks at George and John.

"What?" John asked defensively. "A little variety is good. It gets us more fans."

"But we can't dilute the product," Milo emphasized.

Everyone turned to Nick. Was he letting his attraction to Isabella soften him? The band had a hard-rock image. Now, with two of the band members married, they seemed to be morphing into something different. Perhaps Milo had a point. But making music with Isabella was pure magic. Her power over him was sucking away his raw energy. She was an energy sucker. She could be doing some kind of brain fog thing to him. Everyone was staring at him. What had they been talking about?

"I should do a new song with Isabella for the tour," Nick said. "This is our last tour together. One last song."

Nick picked up some empty beer bottles and strode into the kitchen to fetch more. Kris sauntered after him.

"Did Isabella make you watch another musical?" he taunted.

"Yeah. But this one was stellar," he admitted. "I didn't fall asleep once."

Nick had found himself riveted to the story and into the songs. What was happening to him? What a dilemma. Maintain his edge or succumb to Isabella's goddess enchantment. He might as well give up the band and go hand out toys to children on Christmas Eve.

11 *Passionfruit Wine*

"I want to make our last night together special," George said, coming into the bedroom where Tina was packing.

She looked at him, and tears threatened to spill. "I'm going to miss you so much."

Tina went into his arms, and they held each other tightly. She'd feel much better about leaving if they could overcome this wedge between them. But there was still time.

"The band isn't playing in Boston on this tour, but you can visit anywhere along the way. Whatever works for you. We'll be in New York, Philadelphia, Dallas, San Francisco, Seattle, Phoenix and a bunch of other places. I emailed you the schedule."

"Okay," she said into his shirt. "You're coming for the festival, right?"

"I wouldn't miss it." He pulled back to look at her. "It was the first time I kissed you." He pressed his warm lips to hers.

"Oh, George. I love you so much," she murmured.

"Where's your carry-on? I have something for you." He went to his dresser and opened a drawer. He held out three chocolate bars. "They're organic and fair trade. I got you different flavors: chocolate cherry, coconut chocolate, and orange chocolate."

"Oh! Thank you! I love these!" Tina squealed. "The plane ride is so long, but I have some books to read and I'll try to sleep too. I just wish we were going together."

"Me too. Now get dressed. I'm taking you out someplace fancy. I'm going to wine and dine my wife." He grinned.

Tina quickly threw on a lilac sundress and flats. She twisted her white hair on top of her head and put a bit of mascara on.

"What did I do to deserve such a beautiful wife?" George asked.

Tina blushed.

"It's funny that I don't get recognized much," George said. "Nick gets recognized all the time when he goes out now."

"Well, he did that publicity with Isabella last year," Tina said. "And you wear that hat that hides your face. What about the other guys?"

He shook his head. "I don't think they have trouble either. Just Nick. Loren told me he got recognized once at a store. Funny, huh?"

"I'm glad we don't have to worry about that yet," Tina said.

She went to grab her purse and noticed the vase of flowers on the dining table. George had surprised her a few days ago with a vivid bouquet of red roses.

"I'm so lucky." She smiled at him.

He smiled back. "Maybe we should skip dinner."

She gave him a coy look. "You'll have to wait. I'm hungry."

"Okay, wife. I'm taking you to an expensive, trendy place where all the cool people go."

"I don't know if I'm cool enough for that."

"Don't worry. I'm a rock star." George chuckled. "But nobody is cooler than you. You're the new Santa. Except it's a secret. Secret Santa."

Tina couldn't stop smiling and followed him out to the car. The air was still warm, and the sun was just setting. It was balmy. How she loved it here. She could live here all the time. Someday. Someday when their future daughter assumed the role of Santa. Then they'd retire here, as her parents had.

George took her hand in the car and they drove about twenty minutes, watching the sun set to their left. A splash of pink streaked across the sky, deepening until the sun dipped below the horizon.

"Gemma and Loren came here," George said when they pulled up to the restaurant. "They raved about it. I looked online and they have a lot of veggie options and even some organic choices."

"That's great."

Tina waited until the valet opened her car door, and George handed him the keys. The interior of the restaurant had red tile on the floor, black booths and tablecloths, and a shiny silver bar. George had made a reservation, and they were seated ahead of a waiting crowd hovering by the door.

"Gemma told me we should try the passionfruit wine," George said as they perused their menus and the server waited.

"Okay. Let's try it."

George ordered the wine, and Tina searched for vegetarian dishes on the menu. She always ate the same as George when they were together and had discovered many new tasty foods.

"You might like this," George said. "Garlic new potatoes with string beans, edamame, and black bean cakes. You love potatoes."

"Sounds good. What are you getting?"

"I don't know. They have a bean burger or I could get a veggie stew with lentils. I like lentils."

"They also have a vegetable pot pie with tofu." Tina pointed to her menu.

"It's nice to have so many choices." George smiled happily.

The server returned with the wine, and they placed their orders. Tina lifted her glass to sample the chilled pale pink wine.

"Wait," George said. "I want to make a toast. I know we won't be together for our anniversary, but I want to toast to us and our first year of being married."

"And many more," Tina added.

"Yes. Many more."

They clinked glasses, and Tina took a small sip. "Oh, my gosh! This wine is so good."

George nodded in agreement. "I'm not a wine person, and it's a little sweet, but it has a nice full flavor."

Tina couldn't help taking sip after sip, and a warm,

relaxed feeling settled over her.

"Hey, go easy on that." George laughed.

"Why? My husband's a rock star," she said a bit too loudly. "He can afford it. He's sussus... I mean, susseccful." She giggled. "Sussessful."

Tina ordered another glass when their dinners were placed before them. The smell of garlic rose from her plate. Her stomach was growling relentlessly, and she took a big bite of the potatoes.

"This is delicious." She pointed to her food with her fork.

"I'm glad you like it. I wanted this to be a special night..."

"You're special." She grinned, and a bit of potato fell from her mouth. "Oops. Where's the restroom?"

George pointed to the corner of the restaurant.

"I have to walk all the way over there?" It looked so far.

"Are you okay? Do you want me to walk over with you?" George asked. "You drank on an empty stomach."

Tina made a face. "I'm fine."

She felt better when she returned from the restroom, especially since a fresh glass of wine had been placed beside her plate.

"Yummy." She plopped down and took a big gulp. "Everything is so good." She scooped up a forkful of string beans and edamame.

"Have some bread." George held out the basket of thick, sliced bread.

Tina tore off a warm piece and sopped up the garlic sauce on her plate. "Mmm."

George peered at her food. "It looks like they used rosemary. Can I try it?"

"Sure. And I'll try yours." Tina reached over and dunked her bread in his stew. Then she sipped wine, which soaked into the bread in her mouth.

"How is it?" The server stopped at their table.

"Delicious!" Tina enthused.

"Yes, it's very good. Can I get another glass of wine?"

George asked.

"Make that two," Tina said quickly.

"Two glasses." The server whisked away.

"You're not finished with that glass," George said to her.

"Almost." She took another large gulp. "If I didn't have to fly home, we could come here every night."

"Home?" George repeated. He studied her face for a moment. "You don't think of our place as home, do you? You think of the Nor..." He glanced around and lowered his voice. "You think of up there as home."

Tina stopped chewing as her eyes widened.

"*Our* place is your home. Up there is your parents' place, where you grew up," he emphasized.

"It's *my* place now," she mumbled. "That's where I live most of the time."

"That's the problem." George folded his arms.

"You knew all this before we got married," she reminded him.

"Then I guess it's my own fault."

"George." Her mind felt a little fuzzy. "This is our last night. I just want to have a nice night with you."

Why was he suddenly being so difficult?

"Yeah. You're right. I knew what I was getting into." He gave her a weak smile. "I just hate being apart."

"Me too."

"I don't understand why you don't want to take the opportunity if your father..."

Tina shook her head. She couldn't deal with this conversation right now.

"Okay. Sorry. We've been over this." He picked up his fork.

They ate in silence.

***

"Blitzen!" Lisa sang out as they approached the main barn. "Dasher!" Her breath turned to mist and her face felt frozen. "It's hard to talk."

"Save your breath until we get inside," Walter advised. "We can stay warm by the wood stove."

"Oi! Who goes there?" Donner pushed open the wide door. "Walter. Lisa. It's just you. Come in."

They hurried across the crunchy snow and stepped into the cold barn.

"Go on over to the wood stove," Donner said in his Cockney accent, pulling the door closed.

They rushed over to the radiating warmth of the wood stove and held their gloved hands before it.

"How do they stand it out here?" Lisa marveled.

"They like the cold," Walter said.

"Everyone is rehearsing for our play." Donner came clomping over.

"What play?" Lisa asked.

"We usually do an amateur show. Just for our own amusement, you see. It gets a little boring out here sometimes."

"I can't wait to see it," Lisa said.

"It's really just for us. We usually do a talent show the same night you have your Northern Lights Festival, but we're also doing a play this year. It was Rudy's idea."

"Rudolph?" she said.

"Yeah. You know how he loves to do karaoke," Donner said. "He wanted to do a musical, but we voted against it."

"I like musicals," Walter said.

"Rudy sings enough at the pub. He's been such a diva, and Blitzen's never directed before. I'll be amazed if we pull it all together."

"Well, good luck! Or break a leg," Lisa said cheerily.

"Thanks." Donner turned toward the back of the barn. "Hey, Blitz!" he bellowed. "We've got company!"

The ground shook as Blitzen lumbered out from the back.

"Walter, Lisa." He nodded.

"We just wanted to let you know we're back," Walter said, bouncing up and down to keep warm. "Any problems while we were gone?"

"Nope. We got all the mail from the post office. No worse than last year."

"Good," Walter said.

"We've actually been back a few weeks but haven't felt like dealing with work," Lisa confessed.

"Is that true, Walter?" Blitzen looked at him sternly.

"Uh, yes. We just..."

"Good for you, then." Blitzen guffawed.

Walter sighed with relief. "Well, it's cold and we should get back..."

"Oh, one more thing, Walter," Blitzen said. "There was a young woman lurking about."

Lisa and Walter looked at each other.

"Who?" Lisa asked.

"I don't know her. Tall, blonde, skinny thing. She was wandering around outside the building. I think I scared her off."

"Who could that be?" Walter wondered.

"It was probably just that journalist who interviewed Tina last year," Donner speculated.

"She wasn't tall and blonde," Lisa said. "Do you think it was Sonia, Kai's fiancée? She's blonde."

"I don't think she would've come around without Kai." Walter frowned.

"Maybe it was just somebody from town who got lost," Lisa said.

"Everybody in town knows us," Walter said. "It must've been a stranger."

"A *mysterious* stranger," Lisa added.

12 *Not So Perfect*

"Please don't be mad at me," Tina beseeched in the car on the way to the airport. "I don't know why I drank so much last night. It was just so good, I couldn't help myself."

"I'm not mad." George took her hand. It felt warm and strong.

"Well, I'm mad at myself." Tina peered out the window at the early morning sky.

"Don't be. We made up last night, and it was pretty great." He smiled.

"I know, but... I feel like there's something wrong between us still." Tina shook her head at her lack of words to describe the distance she sensed.

"There's no place I'd rather be than with you, and I'm just a little disappointed..." He didn't finish his sentence.

"I'm a terrible wife."

"No, you're not." He squeezed her hand reassuringly. "We just have a tough situation. We knew this going in."

"I love you so much, George. I hope you believe that. You're the perfect husband," Tina gushed.

"I'm not perfect." He shook his head. "I need to work on being more understanding. Maybe I'm being selfish. Your job is important and I'm just being selfish. Forgive me."

"*You* should forgive *me*," she insisted, studying his profile as he drove. "I should probably consider it if my mother brings it up again."

"I'd never ask you to do that."

"But you were willing to quit the band for me."

"That's different. The band would survive without me. We have Loren now." George glanced at her.

"You and Nick started that band together. That's your dream. Besides, Nick would kill me if you left the band."

George let out a laugh. "He'd kill both of us."

Tina smiled. "Then we'd have to hide out at the North Pole. He never comes up there anymore."

"Why is that?"

She shrugged. "He hates it. I guess my father pressured him too much when we were kids. Everyone thought he was the one who would take over, but he never wanted to. He just wanted to escape."

"I never would've met you if he'd stayed."

"I would've been going to college here, so it's possible we would've run into each other."

"Maybe it was fate no matter what." He lifted her hand to his mouth and kissed it.

"Yes. I think so." She looked out the window. "Goodbye, palm trees. Goodbye, beach. Goodbye, sun."

"You make it sound so final."

"I dread going back to the cold, but I look forward to getting back to work. There's so much to do when we start the season. I don't know what I'd do without Walter and Lisa."

"It's great that they go back before you and get things going," George said.

"I know. I haven't even looked at my emails for weeks except the ones from Lisa. Walter always cleans them out for me before I come back."

"The tour schedule will be in your inbox," he reminded her. "Just let me know when it works out for us to meet up."

"This season should go smoothly," Tina said. "The production line has been modernized so we don't need to hire anybody. The IT team has updated all our programs and made things more efficient and we've reallocated more elves to the mailroom to read the letters until we catch up and then they go back to the production line."

"It sounds like you've got it under control," George said.

"Yes. I should be able to get away in a few months." Tina clasped his hand in both of hers.

Everything was going to be okay.

***

Walter sat at his desk, diligently going through Tina's emails.

"How many are there?" Lisa stood beside him, gazing out the window behind them. "I think I see Prancer by the barn. Or is that Dancer? I can't tell them apart from this far away. Oh, there's Rudy. Now Blitzen is coming out."

"There's 188. Not as bad as last year. I'm just going to scan through these quickly and delete the ones I can. Then sort the rest into folders," he said.

"What can I do?" she asked.

"You can walk through the building and make sure all the lights are working and everything looks in order."

"I'm not doing that by myself. This place is too big and creepy when nobody's here."

"Okay. We'll do that later. Did you turn the heat up in Tina's apartment?"

"Yes. I did that when we brought over the food. At least she'll have something to eat when she gets back."

"Good." He stared at the computer screen. "She got a few emails from Jill, the reporter. I'll put them in her personal folder."

"I like her," Lisa stated. "Even though she did an interview outing Tina. Luckily, nobody believed it, huh?"

"Here's an email chain from you and Tina," he said. "I won't read it. I'll just put it in her personal folder."

"We were probably complaining to each other. That's what we do. Vent to each other."

"Lots of vendor emails." He squinted. "Oh, here's one from the engineer who renovated our machinery."

"Jamie."

"Yes. She and her partner, Amy, got married and they're going to Paris for their honeymoon," he said, scanning the email.

"How romantic."

"So they'll be late coming back to work."

"At least they didn't quit. We need them."

"Wait a minute. What's this?" His dark eyebrows drew together.

Lisa turned from the window and looked over his shoulder. "What is it?"

"It looks like an email from…" He rubbed his eyes and looked back at the screen.

"Skyler Rose! She's a famous singer," Lisa said in amazement. "She does some acting. We saw her in that movie the other night. Why would she be contacting Tina?"

She and Walter gaped at each other and looked back at the email.

"She read the article about Tina and wants to option the rights for a movie," Walter said.

"Shut up!" Lisa shrieked.

"Do you think this is really from her?" he asked. "Wouldn't she have an agent or someone who would do this for her?"

Lisa gasped. "Walter, she's tall and thin and has blonde hair."

"No!"

"Oh, my gosh! She wants to play Tina." Lisa started pacing with excitement. "Who do you think should play me in the movie?"

"Tina won't do it."

"You don't think so?" Lisa stopped.

"If you think that article is bad, just imagine all the tourists who would flood this place if they did a movie."

"You're right." Lisa sighed with disappointment. "But you never know. She did an interview with Jill and let her write an article. I never thought she'd do that."

"Yes. That was a surprise," Walter admitted. "Now we know who our mysterious stranger is."

"Walter." Lisa grabbed his shoulder. "She could still be in town."

***

"Isabella," Nick said into his phone. He liked the musical sound of her name.

"Hi, Nicky," she said in her singsong voice.

"Uh..." His mind emptied.

"Yes?" she purred.

"So, I was thinking, since this is going to be our last tour and all that, we should write one more song together," he proposed. "For the tour. For the fans."

"I was thinking the same thing."

"Right." Why hadn't he waited and let her come to him?

"But I know what you really want," she breathed.

"What?"

"You really just want to spend time with me, don't you?" She laughed lightly.

How could she see right through him like that?

"It's about the fans and what's good for the show."

"Okay, if you insist." Isabella laughed again. It was irritating.

"So, like, we should make some kind of statement," he continued.

"You mean about this being our last tour together?"

"No. Like about the state of the world and how we need to mobilize the masses and start a revolution in the streets."

"Nicky, you know I don't do that type of music."

"But you said I was stretching you musically. Now's your chance to take a stand."

"It's true that our songs have a little more relevance, but you know I'm nonviolent. I'd be happy to do a song promoting peace and love in the world. That's what we should put out there."

"Open your eyes," he blurted. "Passivity doesn't change things. Only revolution..."

"Nicky, you don't have to sell me like one of your fans."

"I mean everything I say on stage."

"I know you do, but it's also your image. You don't have to sell me. I know you. The real you."

Did she? Could she see right into him?

"We're doing a song about hope and peace and love. Something uplifting," Isabella asserted.

"Right," he mumbled.

"And since this will be our last tour together, I think we should do something special to cement our connection, something to bond us while we're apart, don't you?"

"Uh..."

What did she mean by that?

"You know I love your intensity, your passion. It makes me feel..."

Was she finally ready to surrender to her true feelings for him and confess that she couldn't live without him?

Isabella sighed. "I'm going to miss you, Nicky."

"What about the cement thing?" he pressed.

"Our last song."

"Okay."

"I have another musical I think you might like as much as the last one," Isabella said.

"The last one didn't suck," he admitted.

"I'm glad you liked it. We can work on the song and then I'll make dinner and we can have popcorn with the movie."

"When?" Nick tried to sound casual.

"I'll text you."

An entire day and evening with Isabella. It would probably be their last time together before their last tour. It was now or never.

13 *On the Boardwalk*

"I think we should look for her," Lisa said, tapping her nails on the small round wooden table in their kitchen.

Walter shook his head. He cupped his warm mug in his hands. "It's up to Tina to decide how to handle this."

"But she's on a plane right now, and Skyler Rose might be gone by the time she gets back."

"We don't know how Tina wants to handle it."

"Skyler Rose," Lisa said with awe. "I can't believe it."

"Don't get all excited," Walter warned. "Tina's going to tell her no."

"What was that movie we just saw her in?" Lisa furrowed her brow in thought.

"I don't remember seeing her in a movie."

"That's because she had a small role. She's just breaking into acting and is probably looking for something she can star in."

"Jill's the one who wrote the article. I think Skyler has to option it from her," Walter reasoned.

"Didn't Tina get some emails from Jill?" Lisa asked. "Maybe that's what they were about."

"Could be."

"Maybe they need Tina's permission, too."

"She has a pretty voice." Walter sipped his coffee.

"Yeah, and I bet she could play Tina if she colored her hair white," Lisa said.

"Tina won't..."

"She's prettier than Tina. In a different way." Lisa picked up her mug for a sip.

"She's taller."

"She has really pretty eyes, doesn't she?"

"I never noticed her eyes," Walter said.

"She's older."

"They can fix stuff like that with makeup."

Lisa looked at him and laughed. "Walter, you're so funny."

"Well, they do wonders with makeup in movies nowadays."

"Let's go look for her." Lisa pushed back her chair. "It'll be fun and we might never get another chance to meet her."

"She could be feeling lost and confused," he said.

"Yes! She needs our help. She's just a stranger wandering around the North Pole. She could be out there somewhere freezing, for all we know." Lisa jumped up. "Let's go right now. I'll get ready."

Walter shook his head. "We shouldn't get involved."

Lisa pointed her finger at him. "You're in charge when Tina's gone. We need to handle this."

"She probably went back to Hollywood or wherever she's from by now." Walter rose from his seat.

"I knew you'd want to do this." Lisa giggled giddily.

"I'm only doing this to shut you up."

"We'll track her down like detectives," Lisa planned. "We already figured out who the mysterious stranger was by putting clues together."

"That's because there was an email with her name."

"We can find her." Lisa pulled on her boots.

Walter nodded. "It won't be that hard. There aren't that many places she could be around here."

"We'll start at the Snowed Inn & Pub."

"She's either there or at the Kringle Café."

"We'll question people. I'll bring a pad of paper." Lisa clomped over to the desk and pulled open a drawer.

"I can just use my phone." Walter held it up.

"Whatever. Let's hurry before she gets away."

***

"Myra, I'm so glad you and Marty are back from your cruise," Clara said. "Nicholas was driving me crazy."

They lounged on a bench on the boardwalk, wearing straw hats and sunglasses while they people-watched. Gulls swooped down and pecked at bits of food in the sand. The waves crashed lazily on the shore and people strolled on the sand or along the boardwalk.

"I don't know why you didn't come with us," Myra said. She took a cookie from the container that Clara offered. "These are still warm. Did you just make them?"

"Yes. I try to keep his sweet tooth satisfied," Clara said. "But I use healthier ingredients like whole wheat flour, coconut oil, and coconut sugar."

"Clever. You'll have to give me the recipe."

"I'll write it down for you later," Clara promised. "Anyway, he just didn't want to go. What are you going to do?" She bit into a cookie.

"Next time, we should just go by ourselves and leave the guys at home." Myra nudged her.

"Don't I wish."

They smiled as a young woman walked by pushing a stroller. A baby was shaking a teething ring and gurgling loudly.

"How are your grandchildren, Myra?" Clara asked, chewing.

"They grow so fast. My grandson will be in third grade and the little one is starting kindergarten this year." Myra broke off a piece of cookie and popped it in her mouth.

"Goodness! Already?"

"I know. It seems like she was just born."

"I don't think Nick will ever have kids."

"He could surprise you."

"I doubt it. I can't imagine it."

Myra reached for another cookie. "But Tina will."

"Yes, Tina will, but it won't be for a while. She wants to wait until she and George are living together full time."

"I don't blame her. When do you think that will be?"

"Who knows?" Clara shrugged.

Myra brushed her short red hair from her eyes. "It's breezy today."

"It feels good." Clara let out a big exasperated sigh.

"What is it?"

"I just don't know what to do. I don't think Nicholas was ready to retire." She looked at Myra through her sunglasses. "He misses it."

"He seemed pretty burned out to me." Myra peeked into the container and chose another cookie.

"He was, and the stress really got to him."

"You did the right thing, Clara, in making him retire after his heart attack. It was good for his health. Look at all the weight he's lost. He looks so much better, and I bet he feels better."

"I know, but now it's been a few years, and he's ready to go back." Clara gazed out at the ocean.

"Why don't you go up again and help for a few months like you did last year?"

"We will, but I think it made him realize how much he misses it. I could just see him itching to get into that sleigh."

"But you can't take it away from Tina. It's been good for her and she made all those changes that should have been done years ago."

"I know. I was hoping she might want to take a break for a few years. She could go back to college and spend some time with her husband." Clara waved her cookie as she spoke. "It would be nice for her to get back to her life for a while."

"Did you ask her?"

"I brought it up, but it didn't seem like she was interested." Clara shook her head.

"Too bad."

"I don't know how to convince her."

"Maybe you shouldn't. It's not really fair to her," Myra said. "Just when she gets everything going, you take it out from under her."

"You're right. I'm just surprised at her. She usually does what we ask. Nick was always the difficult one."

"I remember." Myra laughed softly.

Clara smiled and brushed crumbs off her lap.

"Just let it go, Clara," Myra advised. "Everything has worked out other than Nicholas is a little bored.

He'll just have to adjust."

"You're right. I'm sure I'm overreacting."

"Don't worry so much. You're retired now. Things will settle. Life goes on."

Clara sighed. "I suppose so."

Myra reached for another cookie. "Are you sure these are healthy?"

"We're getting healthier by the minute," Clara teased.

***

Tina leaned her head back in her seat and turned to look out the window of the plane. If the flight wasn't so long, she and George could see each other more often. They needed to spend more time together. She knew that. It had been a problem since they'd met. But what could they do about it?

Everything had been fine until she'd mentioned the conversation with her mother. Why had she done that? George had always been so patient and understanding about their situation, but now she felt like she had hurt his feelings. She couldn't bear the thought. Yet she shouldn't feel guilty about her job. What did he expect her to do?

It was always unbearable to be apart. It was so unfair that she couldn't have him and her job at the same time. She always felt like she was choosing one at the expense of the other. At one time, he had offered to leave the band so they could be together all the time. Of course, she had insisted that he stay with the band. He loved playing music. She couldn't expect him to give up doing what he loved. Why wouldn't he extend the same consideration to her?

It would be nice to get home. She felt most comfortable there. Now that Lisa had moved in with Walter, she had the place to herself. She was looking forward to a drama-free zone and some peace and quiet. It was nice to be able to lounge around and read. She had a bunch of books on her Kindle just waiting for her. If only George could be there with her, it would be perfect. Otherwise, she'd have to endure the little ache that lingered in her heart whenever they were apart. That was the thing.

Tina was looking forward to an uneventful season. Hopefully, her mother wouldn't bug her anymore about letting her father take over the business. She had to stand firm. She didn't want to lose all the progress she'd made over the past few years. It hadn't been easy. There had been many challenges, but she had persisted and she wasn't about to give it all up.

Of course, it'd be nice to have more time with George and be able to attend classes in person instead of online. But what if her father changed things and undid what it had taken years to accomplish? She didn't want to take that chance and lose all she had achieved. Besides, she enjoyed her job. Truth be told, she loved it and didn't want to let it go.

It would be nice to see Lisa again, too. She missed her friend. Lisa and Walter would have everything ready to go for the new season. Her email would be cleaned out and she could get right to work. First thing, she'd have Lisa set up a meeting with the leads of each department and she'd check in with the reindeer. Blitzen always expected it.

And she had to see Gerta. Gerta would give her some clarification and insight. Tina always came away feeling more lucid and calm. That was exactly what she needed. And a Peppermintini or two.

14 *Clues & News*

Lisa scanned the blindingly white flat landscape as they whizzed along on the snowmobile. Her tinted goggles muted the glare, and she clung to Walter while searching for any sign of color stuck in the snow. Skyler Rose had most likely taken a snow taxi, but there was still a chance she'd gotten lost. It was easy to do in this vastness, unmarked by signs or any obvious landmarks to tell you where you were. It had taken her some time to learn to navigate with a compass. They weren't in Florida anymore.

Lisa tapped Walter on the shoulder when she spotted something to their right. Her mouth was covered by the scarf wrapped around her lower face and neck, but she pointed with a mittened hand. They curved over in that direction. She had to admire Walter's snowmobile maneuvering skills.

"Just a scarf," he yelled. He turned off the motor. "Let's pick it up and turn it in at the Lost & Found at the pub."

Lisa snatched it off the ground and fumbled to open the back compartment on the snowmobile. It was quite difficult with her thick mittens, but she managed to flip the clasp and throw it in before the wind whipped over to snatch it.

They continued on their way. Up ahead, there was movement, causing the ground to tremble beneath them. Lisa squinted until she could make out a herd of reindeer dashing in the same direction. Lisa had never seen them in movement like this, other than the night they pulled the sleigh into the sky. It was a thing of beauty to witness the graceful galloping of these huge, powerful animals. How lucky was she to see things like this?

A few scattered stout houses appeared, each with smoke curling up from its chimney. Snow covered the roofs and long icicles hung down, glinting in the fading sun. The yellow lights of the town beckoned in the distance. Lisa couldn't wait to get inside where it was warm.

Walter parked in front of the Kringle Café. He thought Skyler would most likely be staying there. They hurried inside and stamped the snow off their boots in the foyer. Lisa pulled off her mittens and unwrapped her scarf. She felt like a mummy. The cold always made her irritable and her stomach gurgled.

"Walter." She grabbed his arm. "I'm hungry."

"We just ate," he protested.

"I just want... a warm piece of pie."

"With a scoop of ice cream?"

She shivered. "No ice cream. Maybe hot chocolate."

"Okay."

They went inside and headed over to a table. They ordered two pieces of warmed pecan pie and hot chocolate. As they handed their menus back to the server, Walter asked her if she'd seen Skyler Rose.

"Yes, I have," she replied enthusiastically.

"You have? When?" Lisa asked with surprise.

"Yes, when I went back to visit my sister in Chicago. She took me to a concert for my birthday. It was so cool."

Lisa pulled her pad of paper from her pocket and wrote it down. "Chicago," she muttered.

"And that was the only time you saw her?" Walter asked, frowning at Lisa.

The server tilted her head. "I think I saw her in a movie once."

"Was it that movie on a spaceship? What was the name of that movie?" Lisa asked.

"It wasn't on a spaceship. It was about a bank teller who was held hostage during a robbery," she answered.

"Oh, we haven't seen that one," Lisa said to Walter.

"Anything else?" She smiled.

"No, thanks," Walter said, and she went to get their orders.

"Bank teller," Lisa said out loud and wrote on her

pad.

"That's odd," Walter said, smoothing his beard. "Maybe Skyler Rose wasn't here. She sent that email, but it could've been someone else snooping around the building."

"Someone else." Lisa wrote.

"Why are you writing all this insignificant stuff down?" he asked.

"There are no insignificant clues." Lisa closed her pad.

Walter shook his head. "Whatever. As soon as we finish our pie, we'll head over to the Snowed Inn & Pub and question people there."

*****

Tina hung up her coat and placed her boots neatly side by side in the closet. She wheeled her carry-on into the bedroom and flipped the switch on the gas fireplace as she passed. Thank goodness Lisa had remembered to turn the thermostat up. She donned a light blue pair of sweats and a red sweatshirt before going into the kitchen to find something to eat. Soup. Perfect. She scooped it into a pot and turned the burner on. And there were even fresh rolls.

She returned to the bedroom and unpacked. Then she collapsed on the couch. Oh darn, the soup! She went to check it. Still not warm enough. She turned up the burner and dialed Walter's home number on the wall phone. Voicemail picked up.

"Hi. I just got back," Tina said. "Thanks for turning up the heat and buying me some food. I'm going to eat and go to sleep. I'm exhausted. I'll see you tomorrow."

She texted George. She'd also email him tomorrow. Cell service was so unreliable here. She'd call her mother from her office phone tomorrow. Hopefully, she wouldn't bring up the thing about her father again. If so, she was going to stand her ground. But right now, she was too tired to even think about it. Why was there always something wrong?

Tina poured the soup into a soup mug and smiled as she noticed little pasta alphabet letters in the tomato broth. Lisa had bought her alphabet soup. She sat on the couch and placed her roll on a plate beside her on the couch. She pointed the remote at the TV and flipped through channels to find something that would hold her interest while she ate. She stopped at a talk show. The audience was laughing.

The blonde guest shrugged. "My dress was too tight. What can I say?"

"Now tell us the truth," the host urged. "Are you two involved?"

She smiled coyly and shrugged. "We've been close friends since we worked together."

"I'll take that as a maybe," he said as the audience snickered. "Does this mean you're through touring?"

"Not at all," she answered. "I still intend to do concerts and make albums. I just like to try new things and I enjoy acting. Why not?"

"So what's next for you?" the male host asked his guest.

"I can't really say just yet, but I'm working on getting the rights to a very interesting story and I'm hoping to star in it," she teased. "I've been studying acting in New York and I think I'm ready for this."

"What more can you tell us?"

"All I'll say is that I'm taking a trip up north to see if I can secure the rights."

"Up north? Like Vancouver?"

She laughed lightly. "That's all I can say right now except..."

Tina changed the channel. She stopped at an old black and white movie. She dunked her roll into her soup and took a big bite. It was so good to be home. She couldn't wait to crawl into her nice warm bed and sleep for about twelve hours.

***

"Do you recognize any strangers?" Lisa asked when they entered the busy pub.

"If they were strangers, I wouldn't recognize them." Walter frowned.

"You know what I mean. Do you *see* any strangers?"

Walter stood surveying the patrons.

"The reindeer are over there," Lisa pointed. "We could ask them..."

Somebody bumped into Walter from behind. "Oh, sorry," an older man said as he sidestepped Walter to get inside.

"Fritz," Walter said. "My fault. I'm blocking the door."

"Come on. Let's get a booth before they're full." Lisa tugged his arm.

"I can't believe I let you talk me into this. She's not here. She's probably never even been up here," Walter grumbled.

"I see someone blonde over there." Lisa craned her neck.

"Where?"

She nodded toward her right.

Walter searched for a blonde head. "That's just Sonia and Kai." He gave a brief wave and Kai waved back. "I want to head home after we have a drink, okay?" They slid into a booth.

"Fine." Lisa sulked. She got out her pad of paper. "Walter is no fun."

"Stop with the paper."

Lisa looked thoughtful. "It had to be her. Who else would skulk around the building when it's closed for the season?"

"Skulk?" He raised his eyebrows.

"I'm going to ask the reindeer if they've seen anyone, and then I'll go get our drinks," she said.

"Okay." He watched her navigate her way through the crowd.

"Walter."

Kai had come over and stood next to the booth. He wore a green beanie hat over his long blond hair and a matching scarf draped around his neck. His gray coat was unbuttoned and hung just below his knees.

"Hello, Kai. Nice to see you." Walter looked up at him.

"Would you and Lisa like to join us?"

Walter smiled at the friendly gesture. "Oh, no thanks. We're just having a quick drink and then we're off to go home."

"Okay. We're right over there if you change your mind." He pointed. "I'm heading to the men's room."

Through the milling crowd, Walter saw Lisa conversing with the reindeer. Blitzen shook his head, and she made her way over to the bar. She leaned over and spoke to the bartender who was busily making their drinks. He watched while she talked to a man in a blue and white checkered flannel shirt sitting at the bar. She was friendly and comfortable having a conversation with almost anyone. He wished he felt that at ease with people. He glanced down at his phone to see what time it was, but it appeared to be off. He held it up and moved it around, searching for a signal. Maybe by the window.

Lisa set their drinks down on the table. Fritz stood beside her in his blue and white flannel shirt, holding a beer. Walter looked at him in confusion.

"Fritz drives the snow taxi," she said.

"I know," Walter answered.

"I asked him if he picked up any fares with long, blonde hair and he said yes," she relayed excitedly.

Walter turned to Fritz. "When?"

"Tonight." Fritz chugged his beer. "But I'm off now."

"We don't need a ride home. We have the snowmobile," Walter said.

"Was she tall?" Lisa asked.

"She was sitting down."

"Did you recognize her?" Lisa asked, getting out her pad.

"Yeah. Of course."

"I knew it!" Lisa exclaimed.

"What was her name?" Walter asked anxiously.

"Tina."

"What about Tina?" Lisa questioned. She scribbled on her pad. "Did she ask about Tina?"

"No, she wasn't looking for Tina..." Fritz said slowly.

"Then why did you...?" Lisa tilted her head.

"It *was* Tina. I dropped Tina off." Fritz took a gulp of beer.

"Tina's back? I thought she wasn't coming back until Tuesday." Lisa closed her pad.

"It *is* Tuesday," Fritz said.

"I thought today was Monday."

Walter sighed. "Thanks, Fritz. Sorry to bother you."

"But Tina's hair is white," Lisa protested.

"I guess you're right." Fritz turned to go and then turned back. "Come to think of it, there was this other lady. She had long blonde hair."

"Who was it?" Lisa asked.

"It was... what's her name?" He looked at the floor, thinking. "You'll know who it is."

"It was probably Sonia," Walter said.

"No. It wasn't anybody from around here. My daughter has her CD." He waved his beer around. "That singer."

Lisa gasped. "Oh, my gosh! Skyler Rose!"

"That's the one." Fritz nodded. "That was going to bug me all night."

"Where's she staying?" Walter asked.

"That place by the airport, but she wanted me to drive her around," he said. "She was real interested in seeing the Claus family business. I told her it was closed for the season, but she wanted to have a look, anyway. She even got out and walked around." He shrugged.

"We have to go find her," Lisa told Walter urgently.

"That's a long way. I think we should wait until tomorrow after we talk to Tina. Then we can all go..."

"She's gone," Fritz said.

"Gone?" Lisa turned to him.

"She left on Sunday," Fritz informed them. "But I got her autograph for my daughter."

15 *Last Chance*

Nick took a few deep breaths before he rang the doorbell. He listened to the musical chiming and heard footsteps. Funny, he never heard Isabella walking across the floor because she was always barefoot.

The door was flung open, and Nick involuntarily took a step back. A stern older woman with short dark hair glared at him.

"Yes?"

"Isabella," was all he could say.

"Are you Nick? Come in." She opened the door wider.

He stepped in and removed his shoes. He noticed the dark clogs on her feet and wondered if she was Isabella's housekeeper or perhaps Isabella had hired a new assistant, but why hadn't Isabella asked her to take off her shoes too?

"Nick."

He swiveled his head toward Isabella's voice. She wore her usual loose yoga pants and an oversized top hanging off one shoulder.

He stepped past the woman and approached Isabella. She looked tired and her expression was solemn. Had someone died? He glanced back at the woman who watched them.

"Nick, this is my mother, Ilene," Isabella said. "Mother, this is Nick."

"Hey." Nick couldn't help staring at her. There was no discernible resemblance other than the hair color.

"I don't like your music." Ilene crossed her arms. "Awful. Vile."

"Mother, Nick is just expressing his frustration with society and advocating change..."

"He's promoting anarchy," she snorted. "I don't know why your manager thought you should tour with that terrible group."

"Robin is an excellent manager. He knows what he's

doing," Isabella responded calmly. "We'll be working in the living room."

She turned, and Nick followed her. He sat on the couch and Isabella sat beside him. She leaned toward him.

"She just showed up. She does that. She never calls," she whispered.

Ilene came in and stood with her hands on her hips. "I don't think you should write with him. He's corrupting your ideals, Ilene."

Nick was confused. Why was Ilene talking to herself out loud?

"He doesn't know." Ilene smirked. "Her real name is Ilene, you know. Ilene Bella. Ilene after me and Bella after my mother. She changed it to Isabella. She thinks it sounds theatrical or something."

"Mother!" Isabella said with exasperation. She glanced at Nick with embarrassment. "I thought it was a prettier name." She glared at her mother. "*And* I wanted my *own* name!"

Ilene raised her hands in the air. "I guess you need all kinds of tricks when you don't have much talent. You're not a strong singer. I keep telling you that, Ilene. You need lessons."

"I know. I know. Now please just let us work," Isabella beseeched her.

Ilene shrugged and clomped out of the room.

Isabella slumped back on the couch. "Sorry, Nick. I've been so distracted since she got here. I forgot about our plans until I heard the doorbell."

Nick wasn't sure what to say, though he noticed her distress. "Right. No prob."

Isabella stared at him for a moment expectantly. What could he do? He'd never had trouble dealing with his own parents. He just ignored them and did what he wanted. What was all the drama about?

She sighed and picked up the notebook and pen from the coffee table. "Our last song. What should we call it?"

"Last song," he repeated, thinking.

"Of course! That's brilliant, Nick," she said. "Last Song," she wrote.

"I need some paper."

His creativity flowed better when he could write stuff down and cogitate on it. She tore a page from her notebook and got up to retrieve a pen and a magazine for him to lean on. He watched her fluid movements. What a bummer that her mother was there, ruining their opportunity to be alone and cement their bond. What that meant, he wasn't sure, but it sounded good when Isabella had proposed it.

"Here you go." Isabella handed him a pen, and their fingers touched, sending a little jolt through him.

Nick grabbed the magazine from the coffee table and began jotting on the paper.

"You come up with things fast," she said. "What are you writing?"

"'Last Song by Nick Klaus and Isabella...'"

"Oh, I thought you were already writing lyrics."

"I have some in my head. I just have to get them out." He furrowed his brow. Sometimes the words came so fast, he couldn't keep up.

"*Last song, last touch, last kiss, last lunch...*" he wrote and shook his head, scowling. He scribbled it out and glanced at her.

"*Last song, last glance, last words, last chance...*" he wrote. Last chance.

Was she aware that she could lose her last chance with him? After this tour, they'd go their separate ways. Somewhere down the road, when she was alone at night after a show, she'd think of him and realize she'd blown it.

"Got anything?" Isabella asked, shaking him from his reverie. She peeked at his paper before he could stop her. "Hmm. I like it."

They were sitting so close that their legs were touching. He couldn't take his eyes off her. A long strand of dark hair draped over her shoulder brushed his arm. She lifted her eyes, and he saw something he hadn't seen before. Big vulnerable eyes, like a little girl's. Unguarded, pure emotion pooling within. She couldn't hide herself from him any longer. A faint, musky vanilla scent intoxicated him. He leaned toward her to accept what he saw in her eyes.

"What are you doing?" Isabella asked. "We're working."

"Right." Nick tilted his head downward, focusing on the words he'd written. *Last chance.*

***

Tina padded down the long hallway in her pink fuzzy slippers. She wore jeans and a pink sweatshirt. Her hair was pulled into a ponytail and she yawned as she turned on the light in her office. She seated herself in the big cushioned chair that had conformed to her father's body and turned on the computer. She yawned again as she entered her password. In a few minutes, she'd peek into Walter's office next door and let them know she was here.

Lisa burst into her office, startling her. "You're back! Have you read your emails yet?"

"I just turned on my computer."

"Welcome back, Tina." Walter lingered in the doorway holding a mug. He shook his head at Lisa.

"What?" she said to him.

"Thanks, Walter. Is there a problem or something?" Tina asked.

"You're not going to believe it!" Lisa squealed.

"Which emails should I look at?" Tina squinted at the computer.

"Skyler Rose," Lisa blurted.

Tina looked up. "What about her? I just saw her on TV last night. She was on a talk show."

"Check the emails in your personal file," Walter advised.

Tina opened the file and scanned it. "Aw. Jamie and

Amy got married."

"Read the ones from Jill," Lisa said.

Tina peered at her computer. Her eyes suddenly widened.

"That journalist, Jill, says Skyler Rose wants to option her article for a film. Oh, my gosh!"

"I know. Right?" Lisa giggled. She glanced under the desk. "Are you wearing slippers?"

"Yes, I'm hardly awake. I couldn't sleep last night because I was thinking... well..." Tina let her voice trail off.

"Okay. Who do you think should play me in the movie?" Lisa asked. "If Skyler plays you, we have to find somebody else who's tall. Someone pretty with reddish hair like mine."

"It's Jill's article, so the magazine must own the rights." Tina pressed her lips together. "I wonder if they could do it without my consent. I don't think Jill would do that, though."

"Without your consent?" Lisa sat down. "Darn. I was hoping you'd want to do it."

"Told you," Walter said.

"Lisa, you know I can't agree with this," Tina said. "As much fun as it sounds... oh, wait. I got an email from Skyler Rose!"

"Can I read it?" Lisa ran around her desk and peered over her shoulder.

"What does it say?" Walter asked.

Lisa looked up after a moment. "She sounds really nice. She said she's coming up here and wants to talk to Tina about it. She said she wants to be sensitive to any concerns she has, and that she understands the need for privacy."

"Jill must've told her where we are." Tina bit her lip. "I wish she would've asked me first."

"Jill sent that email a while ago," Lisa said. "She probably couldn't wait for an answer."

"Skyler Rose has already been here and gone," Walter told Tina.

"She has?"

"She left on Sunday," Lisa said. "Blitzen told us he saw someone poking around before we got back."

"Did you meet her? Did anybody from town talk to her?" Tina asked.

"Fritz seems to be the only one. She was staying down by the airport," Walter said.

Tina nodded. "I'll just respond to Jill and let her know I don't want Skyler to option it. And then I'll email Skyler and tell her the same thing."

"Nobody believed the article was real, anyway. They'll just think the movie is made up too," Lisa muttered.

"I shouldn't have done that article. This is getting out of hand," Tina said. "They probably don't need my consent to do a movie, but I hope they'll respect my wishes and our privacy." She put her head in her hands. She had the beginning of a headache.

"Do you want me to get you some chai tea?" Lisa offered.

"Thanks, but I think I need coffee this morning."

"I'll get it." Lisa scurried out of the office.

"Anything else I should know about?" Tina asked Walter.

He shook his head. "I'll let you get to it. We'll talk more later."

Tina stared at the landline on her desk. Might as well get it over with. She dialed the phone.

"Hi, Mom. I just wanted to let you know I got here safely," she said when Clara picked up the phone.

"Thanks for calling, Tina." She sighed heavily into the phone.

"What's wrong?"

"Oh, it's just your father. I always seem to be picking up after him."

"Make him pick up after himself."

"Easier said than done. He's driving me a little crazy. I can't get a minute to myself unless he's out golfing with Marty or when he falls asleep watching TV."

"I thought you looked forward to retiring."

"I did, but I never thought we'd retire so young," Clara said. "But I'm not complaining. How's everything there?"

"Fine."

Tina debated whether to tell her mother about Skyler Rose, but decided it was better to wait and see how it played out.

"I hope you have a quiet season," Clara was saying. "And remember, if you change your mind, I'm sure your father won't mind taking over for a few seasons."

"Do you miss it too?" Tina wondered.

"Well, it's been a nice break, but I could adjust."

"But do you miss it, Mom?"

"I suppose I do sometimes. You know how it is. It's a lot of work, but it's also very rewarding."

"Yes, it is."

"The air is different, isn't it? You can almost see it. There's a certain energy in the air. It just feels different up there. I can't quite describe it, but you understand what I mean," Clara said.

"Yes. I can feel it. It's lighter and kind of shimmery and magical."

Tina had never thought about it before, but it was true. The magic in the air could be what compelled her to keep coming back. There was certainly no other place like it, no other sensation like it.

Clara sighed again. "I have to admit I miss that feeling."

16 *Get a Grip*

"Hi, husband," Tina said cheerfully.

"Hi, wife."

The familiar sound of George's voice was comforting and made her want to crawl through the phone and into his arms.

"I miss you," she murmured.

"I miss you too, and I've been replaying the memory of our last night together in my head."

She winced. "I'm sorry I drank too much."

"Not that part. The part after that."

"Oh." She felt herself blush and was glad no one was there to see it. "Yes. That was nice."

"More than nice," he said. "Anyway, only another few months until I can come up there for the Northern Lights Festival."

"How's the tour going?"

"It's okay. There's just a different vibe," George told her. "Nick is kind of moping around and doesn't have the same energy he usually does on stage."

"Why not?"

"Probably because it's our last tour with *Rock Goddess*."

"That's right."

"But Nick and Isabella wrote this great song together that they've been doing called *Last Song,* and the fans love it. It's really heartfelt. I think Nick is kind of heartbroken."

"Hasn't he told her how he feels?"

"I don't think so. You know Nick. He wants her to come to him. It's an ego thing."

"But he might lose her."

"I know."

Tina let out a little groan, placing her hand on her stomach.

"Is your stomach still bothering you?" George asked.

"Sometimes."

"Tina, you can't let stress get to you. How's work? Is there a problem up there?"

"Not really."

"Talk to me," George pressed. "What's bothering you?"

"Nothing, really. I just got an email from Jill Graham. Remember the woman who wrote the article about me last year? Now someone wants to option it for a movie, but I don't think..."

"Did you say a movie?" he asked incredulously. "When did all this happen?"

"I had some emails when I first got back a few weeks ago and I let them know I wasn't interested, but..."

"Why didn't you mention this before?" he asked.

"Because it's not going to happen. I told them I wasn't interested, but, I don't know, maybe they'll do it, anyway. I never should've done that interview."

"It doesn't do any good to worry about it," he said. "Just focus on work and deal with whatever happens when it happens."

"You always say the right thing."

"I don't know about that." George laughed. "So I thought that maybe I'd bring Gemma up with me for the festival. What do you think? Will there be enough room with your parents there?"

"She could stay in Nick's old room, but I don't think my parents will be happy with another person knowing." Tina rubbed her face.

"Well, she keeps saying she wants to visit us. I won't be able to put her off forever."

"But what if she tells Loren? We can't expect her not to if they're in a relationship," Tina reasoned.

"She won't tell anyone if I ask her not to. Besides, she says that she's not in a relationship with him."

"She repeated what we said when we first told her, and what if she tells your parents?" Tina felt a twinge in her stomach.

"She won't. She thought we were joking before, but

once she realizes it's on the level, she won't tell anyone. I promise," he assured her.

"Okay. I trust you." Tina sighed.

Her parents certainly wouldn't be happy about this.

"Maybe you can talk to Nick," George said. "He won't talk to me, but he might talk to you. I just saw him go by in the hallway."

"I can try."

She heard George call out to Nick.

"Here he comes. I love you."

"Love you too, George," she said before Nick got on the phone.

"Hey, Tina," Nick said.

"Hi, Nick. How's the tour?"

"It's cool."

"How do the fans like the new song? I can't wait to hear it."

"It's sick. They're losing it."

"That sounds good," Tina said slowly. "It must be hard for you because this is your last tour with Isabella and..."

"She's not getting it," Nick interrupted. "Like she's had every opportunity, and she's going to blow her chance to cement us."

"She might not know how to tell you how she feels." She humored him. "You might need to be the one to open up that conversation."

"You think?"

"Not everyone finds it easy to communicate their feelings. Sometimes you just have to say what you feel. Say what you need to say."

Tina thought of herself and George. Did she need to confront the discomfort she still sensed between them?

"Things are complicated. We're artists."

"I think everyone struggles sometimes. You know George and I have issues, too. This distance thing is tough. I just don't know what to do about it. I feel so torn." Her voice broke as she felt an unexpected wave of emotion.

"Wow, Tina."

She sniffed stifling tears. "I couldn't stand it if I lost George."

"Are you demented? Get a grip."

Tina wiped her tears with her fingers. "Sorry, Nick. I don't know where that came from. Don't tell George, okay? I'm just under a lot of pressure."

"That job is a killer. Look what it did to Dad and now you're flipping out."

"I guess I just feel guilty about my job. I mean, I really love it. It's just all the other stuff that complicates things." Tina let out a little groan. "Nick, I really hope you can work things out with Isabella. I like her. She's perfect for you."

"I know."

"Can I talk to George again?" she asked.

"I don't know where he went," Nick said.

"Never mind. Just tell him I said goodbye. And talk to Isabella. Be honest with her. Don't play games," Tina advised.

"Right."

***

"Listen," Walter said, closing his office door and seating himself at his desk.

"What?" Lisa followed him. "Are you talking about that squeak? I think it's your chair."

"No. I mean, listen to me. Tina seems really fragile. I don't know what's going on. She could've had a fight with her parents or something..."

"She could've had a fight with George." Lisa's eyes widened. "Is that possible?"

"Whatever it is, something's going on with her. Let's just do everything we can to make things easier for her. I hate to think that this job is getting to her already."

"The first few years were rough because she didn't have the support of her parents and her Uncle Kris tried to take it all away from her," Lisa recalled. "And then

Jill started stalking her to get an interview, and she regrets doing it."

"And now Skyler Rose." Walter rubbed his chin. He'd grown back his beard and was still getting used to it.

"I'll talk to her and see what's up," Lisa said. "I'll let her know we've got her back."

"Tina can be stoic. She holds things in and tries to do what everyone expects."

"I'm surprised she stood up to her parents about Santa coming back," Lisa said.

"That must be it." Walter pointed at her thoughtfully.

Lisa gasped. "I just realized her anniversary is coming up."

"I bet she's depressed that she and George can't celebrate together." Walter nodded. "We have to take her mind off things. You two should have a girl's night out."

"I like that idea." Lisa giggled.

There was a knock on the office door. They looked at each other.

"Come in," Walter called.

Tina cracked open the door and peeked in.

"I don't want to interrupt. Is there a problem?"

"No, not at all," Lisa said. "Walter and I were just making out."

"Lisa!" Walter looked embarrassed. "We weren't. We were just..."

Tina held up her hand. "No need to explain."

"Hey. We should go out. Just us girls," Lisa said. "We haven't let loose for a while. It'll be fun."

"Oh." Tina placed her hand on her stomach. "I was just going to tell you I'm going to go lie down. My stomach is acting up again."

"I hope you're not getting an ulcer," Lisa said.

Walter poked her.

"What?" She poked him back.

"Don't worry," Walter said to Tina. "We'll take care of everything. Take all the time you need."

Lisa trailed behind her. "Do you have any aloe vera juice? Probably not. That would make your tummy feel better. How about a heating pad? Do you have one of those?"

"That's a good idea. I don't know if my parents had one. I'll check the apartment," Tina said. "Sorry, we can't have a girl's night. We'll do it soon."

"We'll just have to drink twice as much," Lisa called after her.

***

"Nick." Isabella beckoned from the doorway of the dressing room she shared with Lilliana. "Lilli hooked up with a roadie," she whispered with a smile.

"Not Kris," he said in horror.

"No way." She waved her hand dismissively. "Some local guy that was helping out."

Good. They were alone. He stepped into the dressing room.

"Hey, Nick," George said.

He was seated comfortably on the sagging couch. Nick ambled in and leaned on a table scattered with colorful scarves and makeup. He tried to mask his disappointment with nonchalance.

"George was telling me how bummed out he is that he can't be with Tina on their anniversary." Isabella made a sad face.

"Right." Nick frowned.

"It's been tough on their relationship." She looked at George sympathetically.

"Yeah. Distance sucks." George stood.

"Don't go, George," Isabella implored. "Let's discuss the show. I think 'Frozen Dreams' might be a better lead-in for 'Last Song' than 'Rock Me.' What do you guys think?"

"Instead of doing 'Last Song' mid-set for us, or even as a lead-in for *Rock Goddess* to come on stage, maybe you could end the show with it," George said.

"Perfect!" Isabella squealed, clapping her hands.

"But what if you do an encore song?" Nick asked.

"You could do it as the encore," George said.

"We'll do something else as the encore song. I want to send them out into the night rocking," Isabella said. "We could all get on stage together and do 'Rock Me.' I always liked that song. It's fun."

"That's a great idea," George agreed. He glanced at Nick before edging toward the door. "I have to go call my parents. I promised I'd call them."

Isabella sighed as he exited. "I really like George. He's such a great guy."

"Right." Nick's mind ricocheted with things to say. He noticed her staring at him.

"Is there something you want to say?" Isabella smiled flirtatiously.

He had to play this right. He couldn't give himself away and let her have the upper hand.

"Hmm." She shook her head. "You never really talk to me other than about music or the set or revolution. Otherwise, you're a closed book. Just say what's on your mind."

Nick looked at her standing there with her hands on her hips and flashed on her mother. He involuntarily took a step back and bumped into a chair.

"Are you scared of me?" Isabella stepped toward him. "You are, aren't you? I intimidate you." She laughed softly. "Oh, Nick. Where's that passion I see on stage?"

And then something snapped. It surged forth and Nick covered the space between them without thinking. He grabbed Isabella. He was going to rock her world.

17 *First Anniversary*

"Is this Santina?"

Tina didn't recognize the crisp British voice on the phone. "Yes. May I help you?"

"Oh, lovely!" she exclaimed. "This is Skyler Rose. I got your email, but I wanted to talk to you directly."

"Oh!" Tina sat up straight at her desk.

"I wish we could've met. This is so impersonal, and I have to admit, I was really hoping to see everything up there at your toy factory."

"I'm sorry I missed you."

"I want you to know I understand your objections," Skyler said. "Jill told me you wouldn't agree to the film, and I was hoping to talk to you in person about it."

"I'm surprised she told you where we are," Tina said. "It's important to keep this place a secret. I don't want people flocking here like some tourist attraction. It would disrupt our work and ruin this small town."

"I completely understand. I have to guard my privacy as well. I haven't told a soul," she said. "I haven't been able to get the backing anyway, but we'd fictionalize everything, of course. A screenwriter would have to embellish and dramatize it."

"In what way?" Tina wondered.

"There would have to be some sort of story. I've been thinking about it and talking to this screenwriter I know," Skyler went on. "I just wanted to meet you and get a feel for the place and the reality before we attempted to imagine a story around it."

"Does the screenwriter know it's real?"

"No, don't worry about that. Everything is strictly confidential," she assured Tina. "I'm still hoping to get this project going and I wanted to base it on the article because I found it so charming. Elves and talking reindeer. How cute is that?"

"Did you talk to anyone while you were here?" Tina asked.

"Everyone was quite mum, though the taxi driver took me round," she said. "I walked around the building a little and saw some reindeer in the back. I didn't realize the place was so huge and I was freezing. I couldn't stay out there for long."

"What kind of story were you thinking of doing?" Tina asked. "I'm just curious."

"Well, I've been looking for a strong female role that would be fun to play, and I told the screenwriter that I want a mix of comedy and drama," Skyler elaborated. "This type of fantasy is better as something not too serious, but I don't want to make a joke of her."

"Her?"

"The Santina character."

"You won't use my name, will you?" Tina asked, with a feeling of dread crawling up her spine.

"Jill used that name in the article."

"True." Tina rubbed her stomach. "But I wish you wouldn't."

"There may not be a film anyway unless I get backing," Skyler reminded her.

"I really would prefer that you don't do this movie, especially if you're going to base it on the article and use my name," Tina insisted.

"Look. I don't need your permission to do this," Skyler informed her. "I was hoping for your cooperation. I respect what you do, and I promise to respect your privacy."

"Thank you," Tina said meekly.

"I don't mean to be harsh. We can change things, even though you have the perfect name. Really. I don't want to upset you. I called because I wanted to reassure you, but I'm not doing a good job of that, am I?" Skyler gave a little laugh.

"I guess if you change my name and don't give away our location, nobody would know..."

"They'll just assume it's made up, like the article. A figment of our imaginations." Skyler chuckled.

Tina absentmindedly wrapped the phone cord

around her fingers. It didn't seem like there was much she could do.

"It sounds like you've decided." She bit her lip.

"Don't worry, Santina. It'll be fine. I give you my word. After all, I don't want to get coal in my stocking, now do I?" Skyler laughed heartily.

"Oh, we don't do that," Tina said quickly.

***

"You're not even touching your Peppermintini," Lisa noticed. They were sitting in their usual booth at the Snowed Inn & Pub.

Tina glanced at the booths by the stage where the boisterous reindeer sat. Rudolph loped up onto the stage and tapped the microphone.

"Test. Testing."

"Is it your stomach?" Lisa asked.

"Now I'm getting a headache," Tina said.

"I know it's your anniversary soon and you miss George…"

"Tomorrow."

"It's tomorrow? I can't believe it's been a year already. Time sure flies." Lisa sipped her Polar Colada. "Where is he? Where's the band now?"

"I don't know. Probably Phoenix." Tina tentatively sipped her drink. Her stomach didn't seem to appreciate it. "I've been drinking too much, anyway."

"We haven't been out once since you got back."

"I drank too much the night before I left and George wasn't happy about it," she admitted. "I ruined our last night."

"You argued the night before you left?"

"We made up that night, but still."

"What did you argue about?"

"We didn't really argue," Tina said. "I could tell he was disappointed that I wouldn't consider letting my father take over for a few years." She tried to sip her drink again.

"That's even worse." Lisa nodded. "You're not considering it, are you? I don't think I want to work for your father. It wouldn't be the same."

"I'm not going anywhere. I just wish everyone would stop pressuring me. It makes me feel so guilty."

Lisa nodded sympathetically. She looked over at the stage.

"Remember when we did karaoke that one night? A bunch of us did 'Girls Just Want to Have Fun.' It was crazy."

Tina smiled. "That was fun."

Lisa glanced at her phone. "We have about half an hour before it gets loud in here."

"Skyler Rose called me."

"What?" Lisa shrieked. "Is she coming back up here?"

Tina took a sip of water and shook her head. "I doubt it. I asked her not to do the movie."

"What did she say?"

"I don't think I can legally stop her. I wouldn't want to do that anyway because of the publicity."

"Good point."

"She said if she finds financial backing, she wants to do it," Tina said.

"Oh, my gosh." Lisa sipped her drink. "It doesn't matter, Tina. Nobody will believe it's real. There's no sense worrying about it."

"That's what George said."

"Though it would be cool to see a movie about us." Lisa giggled. "I can't help it. I think it's cool."

Tina smiled and shook her head.

"Well, it is." Lisa shrugged.

Tina pushed her drink away. "I can't drink this tonight. My stomach is bothering me and I have a headache."

"Let's go back to your place and see if we can find a movie that Skyler Rose is in on demand," Lisa suggested. "Do you have any popcorn?"

Yes, and I found a heating pad. You're right. It

totally helps my stomach," Tina said.

***

"Happy anniversary, wife," George said over the phone.

"George! It's so good to hear your voice." Tina swiveled in her desk chair to look out the window. "I didn't know if you'd be able to call. I thought you might send me an email. Where are you?"

"We just checked into our hotel in Phoenix. I'm wiped out, but I wanted to call you before I crashed."

"I wish we could be together today," Tina said wistfully.

"Me too. It sucks that we can't be together on our first anniversary."

"George, I'm so sorry... you know I love you more than anything and I can't bear to be apart. I just..."

"I know, Tina. You don't owe me an explanation. This is who you are," he said. "It's selfish of me to expect you to give it up for a few years after you've worked so hard to improve everything."

"But I don't want you to think..."

"I don't. Neither of us is ready to give up our careers. I know I said that I'd leave the band and move up there with you, but..." He let out a heavy sigh. "I forget how much I love it. Being on stage is such a rush. Feeling the energy and love from the audience is... I can't describe it."

"Oh, George. I just love you so much."

"That's what I wanted to hear," he said. "I love you too, with all my heart. When can you visit? Maybe L.A.? Gemma might come to L.A."

"Maybe." Tina's stomach twisted and she squeezed her eyes shut.

"Just let me know," George said. "Whatever works with your schedule. It's probably easier to reach me by text or just leave a voicemail."

"How's Nick?" Tina watched the reindeer prance by

the barns. "I'm not sure if it helped when I talked to him on the phone."

"I don't know. Something happened between him and Isabella. The whole chemistry of their duet is off. He won't talk to me about it."

"Oh, no. I encouraged him to tell her how he felt. What did he say to her?" Tina worried as her stomach bubbled.

"I'll see if Isabella will talk to me. We can't have anything affect the show like this," George said. "It feels like the entire show is off. Nobody is getting along."

"That's terrible." Tina covered her mouth with her hand and glanced at the door to her office. "I'm sorry. I have to go."

"Okay. I'm going to crash for a few hours. Happy anniversary," George said. "I love you."

"Love you, too."

Tina slammed down the landline receiver and ran out into the hallway. She held her hand over her mouth until she made it to the restroom. The contents of her stomach erupted and spilled into the toilet. She washed her shaking hands and rinsed her mouth. What was wrong with her? Could Lisa be right that she was developing an ulcer? Now she was really scared.

18 *Drama Trauma*

"She doesn't want to talk to you, Nick." Lilliana held the dressing room door open a crack.

"Right." Nick shuffled from one foot to the other. "We have to talk about the set. Our song."

"Go away, Nick." She shut the door.

Nick stood in the hall, wondering what Isabella expected him to say. He'd only responded to her signals. He was sure he hadn't misread her. That little smile and the way she looked at him. The way she drew him to her with her eyes. Was she still in denial about her feelings? That wasn't his fault.

He meandered until he found Kris by the catering table sniffing sandwiches.

"They have tuna!" Kris announced. "Want some?"

Nick shook his head.

"What's up with Isabella?" Kris asked. "She's got an attitude like she's better than us or something."

Nick shrugged. "Women. Hot and cold, right?"

"That's why I'm single," Kris said. "No drama. I can do whatever I want and I don't have to answer to anybody."

"Right." Nick munched on potato chips.

"There's beer in the dressing room." Kris led the way, dropping crumbs and globs of tuna.

"There he is," Milo declared when they entered. "What's up with you and Isabella?"

"I knew this would happen." John shook his head.

"She's been leading him on." Loren came to his defense.

"Nick, did something happen between you?" George asked.

Nick looked at the guys draped around the room holding beers. All eyes were on him.

"Girls are crazy. That's why I'm single," Kris said.

"You're single because you're pathetic," Milo said.

"I'm single by choice," Kris responded haughtily.

"No, *I'm* single by choice. I'm the only smart one here. You guys are getting sucked in, losing your freedom." Milo circled his finger to encompass them. "You're missing out on all our devoted fans, but now there's more for me."

"Rock-n-roll!" Kris yelled, raising a fist.

"What happened with Isabella?" George asked again.

"Nothing," Nick answered.

"Just fix it," John said. "It's affecting your song together. You always had good chemistry, but it's obvious she's pissed about something."

"She won't talk to me," Nick said reluctantly.

"Something happened," Loren said. "Spill it, man."

"He doesn't have to tell us anything," George said. "It's between them."

"But she won't talk to him," John said. "We can't have tension on stage."

"Do you want me to talk to her?" George offered.

Nick considered this. Women seemed to like George and open up to him for some reason. He didn't get it. But what would the guys think?

"Nah." Nick waved his hand. "She'll get over it."

"It must be a full moon or something," George mused.

"Kris, watch what you're doing. You're making a mess," Milo complained. "Pick up that chunk of whatever you're eating off the floor before someone steps on it."

***

Kai opened the door. His long blond hair hung past his shoulders. "Lovely Tina. Come in. You look..." He frowned.

Tina stepped into the foyer and removed her gloves and boots. He slipped her coat off her shoulders and hung it up on a hook beside the other bulky coats.

"Sonia and I were just planning the wedding with

my parents," he said.

Tina gazed up into his familiar blue eyes. They'd known each other since they were children. Everyone had always assumed they'd marry one day, including her. She felt a great fondness for him.

"Sorry to interrupt," she said.

Kai gave her an affectionate hug. "Do not apologize. You are like family."

"I'm happy for you and Sonia." Tina smiled. "I'm looking forward to your wedding."

"I hope your George will be able to attend."

"Me too."

Kai furrowed his brow. "Are you well? Your face is pale."

"You mean more than usual?" She gave a little laugh, but it was concerning that it was noticeable.

Kai smiled and led her into the toasty warm kitchen. His father, Jann, and mother, Gerta, sat at the long wooden table with Sonia. It was funny that Kai's parents were short and stout while he was tall and thin.

"Tina." Sonia rose and embraced her. "It is good to see you."

Tina always marveled at Sonia's perfection. She looked like a porcelain doll with perfect skin, white teeth, clear blue eyes and straight, silky light blonde hair. She wore a cream-colored cowl-neck sweater and a brown skirt.

"Little Tina." Jann wrapped her in a comforting hug.

"Sit. I have made ginger tea for you, my dear," Gerta said.

"Okay." Tina always looked forward to Gerta's hot chocolate with mini marshmallows, but she gladly accepted the mug of tea.

Everyone discreetly exited the kitchen, leaving them alone.

Gerta shook her head slowly. "You are pale. Tummy problems?"

Tina nodded. "George wants me to visit him on the road, but I'm afraid to fly like this. What can I do? It's getting worse."

"I always warned your father that stress would affect his health. You are like him in this way. The ginger tea will settle your stomach."

"Do you think it's just stress?" Tina asked anxiously.

Gerta smiled and took her hand. She lightly brushed her fingertips over Tina's palm. "Why so much worry?"

The reassuring warmth of Gerta's touch calmed Tina.

"I keep disappointing everyone," she said softly. "My father is bored and wants to come back, and my husband is hurt that I won't let him, so I can go back to Florida."

Gerta nodded. "I knew your father was not ready to retire, but he needed this time off for his health."

"Do you think I should let him come back?" Tina asked.

"This is your decision. You must listen to yourself. Your inner voice is certain. When you listen to everyone else, you cannot hear your own voice. Now be still and calm." She set her palms down on the table.

Tina took a deep breath. "I know what I want but..."

Gerta wagged her finger. "No but. Everyone accepts your decisions."

"I know, but George..."

"Your husband understands."

Tina sighed. "I guess you're right."

"Everyone loves you no matter what you choose." Gerta smiled warmly and handed Tina a cloth handkerchief.

"Oh, Gerta." Tina felt the tears come. "I'm a nervous wreck."

"Trust yourself, my dear."

"But what will my father do?"

"Your father will always grumble about something."

They both laughed while Tina dabbed her eyes.

"I don't want George to think..."

"He does not," Gerta assured her.

Tina took a few deep breaths. Her stomach seemed to settle down.

"Last year, you said that my brother was struggling. Is he okay? George told me that something is going on with him and he won't talk to anybody."

"Nick has his challenges, as we all do." Gerta sipped from a mug. "He will figure things out for himself. You must think of yourself now. Take care of yourself."

Tina took a sip of the warm tea. "There's a singer who wants to make a movie about me. That's another thing I've been worrying about. I can't let that happen, but she wouldn't listen. She said she doesn't need my consent."

"Let it go." Gerta opened her hand and waved her fingers.

"So, it won't happen?"

"You do not control this and it makes no difference."

"But my parents..."

Gerta held up her hand. "My dear, do not give your attention to these things. There is something more important."

"What?" Tina thought. "My health." Her eyes widened. "It's serious, isn't it?"

Gerta nodded. "Yes. You must call your husband and your parents."

19 *Worst Timing Ever*

Nick prowled the backstage area. Isabella had to be here somewhere, preparing to go on for their song. *Black Ice* remained on stage, performing one of John and Milo's songs "Edge of Mind". Afterwards, he and Isabella would sing their duet "Last Song." He had to find her and he only had a few minutes to do it.

"Isabella," he called when he saw her.

Lilliana stepped between them. "She doesn't want to talk to you, Nick."

"It's okay." Isabella approached him.

Lilliana glared at Nick before striding away.

"Why aren't you on stage?" Isabella wondered.

"You like me," Nick blurted.

She yanked him into a corner veiled by long drapes, hidden from view.

"Why did you grab me like that, Nick? I told you we're just friends. I don't get involved with other musicians. I told you that from the start."

"You kissed me before," he reminded her. "More than once."

"For publicity," she emphasized. She shook her head. "All this flirtation is for the fans. They like to think that we're..." She waved her hand between them.

Nick was confused. He couldn't be wrong about this.

"But we have a chemical thing..."

"Chemistry?" Isabella tried to suppress a smile. "We do have chemistry. That's why our duets work."

"Right." His thoughts jumbled, and he tried to sort them out.

"We're too different," Isabella said. "You're... hardcore. Your songs are aggressive. I'm... romantic and gentle. It works when we mix it up on stage but not off stage."

He could hear George playing a guitar solo to give him more time. He was a loyal friend.

"You crossed your signals," Nick accused.

"You got it wrong." Isabella jabbed a finger at him. "You and me? Not going to happen."

"You like me. You can't fool everyone except me." He shook his head. "I mean I know…"

Isabella held up her hand. "Truce, okay? Let's not let this misunderstanding ruin our song." She turned to walk away.

Misunderstanding? Great name for a song, Nick thought. But he hadn't misunderstood. She was still fighting her feelings for him because of a silly rule she had. He knew it deep down.

"You're going to blow it." Nick pointed a finger at her.

Isabella looked over her shoulder at him. He melted on the spot as her eyes once again bore into his soul.

"Sorry, Nicky." A smile played around those soft lips he'd kissed.

***

Tina's mind was racing. She parked the snowmobile and hurried up to the apartment. She had to speak to George first, before anyone else. She wished he were here so they could talk in person. What if she couldn't reach him? What would his reaction be if she did? She paced, wringing her hands. The ginger tea had settled her stomach, and she shouldn't let herself get worked up again.

She grabbed the receiver from the wall phone by the kitchen and dialed George's number. His voicemail picked up.

"George, call me as soon as you get this message. It's important."

Tina realized her hands were shaking as she dialed her office number to reach Lisa.

"Did you see Gerta?" Lisa asked. "I want to go next time."

"Yes, I did. I just called because…"

"What did she say?"

"I'll tell you later. I'm going to take the rest of the day off."

"Is it your stomach again?" Lisa asked. "Did you ask her about that? Isn't she some kind of healer?"

"Kind of. She gave me some tea that helped, but I'm just going to take the rest of the day off." Tina attempted to sound casual.

"Yeah. There's nothing going on today that Walter and I can't handle," Lisa assured her. "Let me know if you need anything."

"I will. Thanks."

Tina went into the kitchen with the little paper bag that Gerta had given her and made ginger tea as she had instructed.

The phone abruptly jangled, startling her, and she hurried to answer it. It must be George! She couldn't wait to hear his comforting voice. Everything would be fine once they spoke.

"Hello?" she said breathlessly.

"I hope I didn't wake you," Clara said. "I called your office and Lisa answered. She said you're sick. Do you have a cold? You know you really need to take more vitamin C and zinc."

"I don't have a cold. My stomach is just bothering me a little."

"You and your father with your stress. You should try meditation. It really helped me, although I haven't meditated lately. That and yoga. Yoga is calming. You should try that too. It's very grounding and keeps you flexible."

"Sounds like a good idea," Tina said.

"I hope you feel better," Clara said. "I just called because I feel bad."

"Why do you feel bad?"

"I feel like I was pressuring you to let your father come back. I still think it would be good for everyone, especially now with your stomach issues..."

"Mom..."

"I'm just saying. Let me finish. Anyway, I feel bad because I know you enjoy being up there and running the business, and I don't want to take that away from you. You've done such a wonderful job and made so many improvements. I was quite impressed when we were up there last year. I want you to know that."

"Thanks, Mom. I'm glad you feel that way."

"You know how I worry about the family. I want everyone to be happy," Clara continued. "But it worries me that you're already having so many stomach issues. That's not good. You should go see Gerta. She knows all these natural remedies."

"Good idea."

"Your father would never listen to her. You know she warned him for years about his health, but he never listened. You know how stubborn he is."

"Yes, he is."

"I can't tell you how frustrating that is. Just yesterday, I asked him to vacuum. He argued with me, insisting that I had just vacuumed, so I said no, it was weeks ago. How could he not see stuff on the rug?" Clara asked. "I'm trying to get him to do more around here instead of expecting me to do everything while he sits in front of the TV like a lump. It's like pulling teeth."

"Did you get him to vacuum?" Tina wondered.

"He finally did it this morning. I think he actually felt proud of himself." Clara laughed. "Small steps, I guess."

"That's good."

"You're lucky that your husband cooks. I bet he cleans up after himself, too."

"Yes, George is great," Tina agreed. "Mom, I think I'm going to get off the phone so I can lie down. I'm a little tired."

"Are you having trouble sleeping? Now, what did Gerta tell me to give your father for that? You should ask her."

"I will."

"Okay. I want you to remember that if it gets to be

too much or you need a break, your father can take over for a little while, okay? Just for a season or two."

"I know, Mom. Say hi to Dad."

They hung up. Tina stared at the phone, willing George to call. It felt awful keeping things from her mother, but she had to tell her husband first. In the meantime, she had to remain calm.

***

Some of the tension between Nick and Isabella on stage seemed to have dissipated, to the great relief of both bands. Once again, their bantering and body language during their duet had become playful and flirtatious. Nick couldn't wait until things returned to normal offstage as well.

He wasn't sure what had gotten into Isabella. Her unspoken signals had been loud and clear. She wanted him. She was finally projecting that affirmation to him, and he certainly wasn't going to ignore it. Maybe her consciousness hadn't aligned with her subconscious yet. Or maybe she still fought her feelings for some obscure reason. Nick couldn't help wondering if it had to do with her mother and her childhood. Had her parents messed her up like his had?

"Hey." Nick motioned to Isabella.

She dallied by the food table, laughing with Lilliana and Kris. Lilliana shook her head at Isabella, but Isabella turned toward him with a faint smile. She enjoyed tormenting him. He just knew it. He walked away from everyone and she trailed behind him.

"I'm trusting you to be woke," she remarked.

"Right." Nick mulled over the right words. "So, is this about your mother and your childhood?"

Isabella stopped and put her hands on her hips. "Excuse me?"

"I get it," he assured her. "My parents messed with my head when I was a kid." He ducked into a dressing room and she slowly followed.

"How?" she asked.

"They piled all this guilt on me. They wanted me to run the family business when my father retired, but I was, like, into my own musical thing. I'm not into business. I'm an artist."

"My mother wanted me to become a music teacher," she admitted. "She put a lot of pressure on me."

"Guilt, man." Nick shook his head.

"It's an albatross."

"A trap."

"Even when *Rock Goddess* became successful, she kept telling me it wouldn't last and I should do something more important with my life," Isabella confided.

Nick bobbed his head.

"But she sure accepts my help financially."

"Right."

Isabella met his eyes. "I've never talked to anyone about this except Lill."

"Your secret's safe with me."

"I believe you." She went over and stood before the window, staring up at the stars in the darkness. "She tells me I can't sing, that I have no talent."

"She's wrong."

Isabella turned to face him. "I can't figure you out, Nick."

"Nothing to figure out." He pointed to his head. "Nothing."

"So now your sister's running the business instead of you. The pressure is off."

"Right. But they really expected me to do it because I'm the son," Nick said.

She nodded. "Patriarchal stereotypes still exist."

"Yeah." He didn't quite get what she meant, but it sounded supportive. "The song was stellar tonight."

Isabella smiled. "I felt more relaxed with you on stage. It's a great song, Nick. The fans went crazy."

"Right."

"Sometimes your words are like poetry," Isabella

mused. "So moving, so emotional, but other times, well... you're too aggressive. You're a paradox."

What was she talking about?

"Pair of ducks?"

"You crack me up." She giggled, covering her mouth with her hand. "But really, what do you have against Christmas? Some of your songs are anti-Christmas and anti-winter like 'Jingle Hell' and 'Frost in My Head.'"

"It has to do with the family toy business."

"But Christmas must've been lucrative for your family. Where's your holiday spirit?"

"That spirit is about greed and materialism."

"I guess you could look at it like that, but I kind of like the holidays. It just seems like a magical time."

"It is. I mean, it depends on stuff."

"Stuff?"

"Like getting stuff. I don't like the whole Naughty or Nice thing either. Kids shouldn't be judged for being kids. The whole holiday is negative. The masses need..."

"Nick?"

"Huh?"

"I hate to admit it, but I'm going to miss performing with you after this tour."

Nick couldn't take his eyes off her. Isabella glanced at him almost shyly. There it was again. That look that beckoned to him. Her words said one thing and her expression said another. Why were her signals all mixed up like this? Why couldn't she acknowledge how she felt about him?

"I probably overreacted," she murmured. "I do like you, Nicky. You intrigue me. Maybe because we're so different. What is it about you?" She took a step toward him.

Nick dared not move. He'd blown it last time. He had to be patient and let her come to him. Why was this room so freaking big?

"Nick." Kris hovered in the doorway.

"We're busy," Nick said tersely.

"But..."

"Not now, Kris."

"But someone's here to see you," Kris said. "You're not going to believe it!"

Nick tore his eyes away from Isabella, who had turned her attention to Kris.

"Who is it?" Nick asked.

Whoever it was had the worst timing ever.

"I can't believe it," Kris gushed.

"Who is it?" Nick asked wearily. "A reporter?"

"It's Skyler Rose!" Kris yelled in a high voice that hurt Nick's ears.

"Did you say Skyler Rose?" Isabella asked with surprise. "Do you know her, Nick?"

"Hurry! She's waiting." Kris scurried off.

"Not yet," Nick said to Isabella and strode after Kris.

20 *Cracker Snacker*

"George," Tina said into the phone. "It's so good to hear your voice." She paced, wrapping the long phone cord around herself.

"I'm sorry I didn't call sooner. It's so crazy here," he said. "Is everything okay? Are you okay?"

"My stomach has gotten worse, and I even threw up."

"Tina, you need to see a doctor. There's something wrong."

"I went to see Gerta..."

"She's not a doctor, is she?"

"No, but my mother told me to see her. She knows how to heal things with herbs and supplements," she explained.

"What did she say? Did she tell you what to do?"

"She gave me some ginger tea..."

"Has it helped?" he asked.

"Yes, but..."

"I know. It doesn't get to the cause. You need to find a way to reduce the stress of your job. I think that's why you get sick sometimes. Stress affects your immune system," George said.

"My mother talked to me about yoga."

"That's a good idea."

"But I don't think stress made me throw up."

"What do you think caused it?"

Tina took a deep breath. "I might be pregnant."

This was the first time she'd said it out loud. There was silence on the other end of the line.

"George?" She bit her lip.

"Have you taken a test yet?" he asked.

"Not yet, but that's what Gerta thinks, and I have all the symptoms. It's probably morning sickness, except I have it all day. Sometimes that happens. I don't know why this didn't occur to me sooner."

"Tina, this is amazing news. I... I don't even know

what to say."

"I think it happened on the last night," she said. "Are you happy about it?"

"Happy? I'm... there are no words for this. Of course, I'm happy. Have you told anyone else? We shouldn't tell anyone until we're sure."

"I wanted to talk to you first. Nobody knows yet except Gerta. She was sure about it and once she said it, I just knew she was right, but I'll take a test," she assured him.

"You should go to a doctor."

"Gerta's a midwife. She delivered me and Nick."

"Okay. Then let me know as soon as you confirm it with a test so I can call my parents."

"I will."

"I'm so happy. We should be together right now. I wish I was there with you."

"Me too."

"Tina, this is the best news I've ever heard. I can't believe it. We made a baby."

"Yes. We made a baby."

Tina realized she had tears running down her face as she unwound herself from the phone cord.

***

"Tina asked me to bring her crackers from the cafeteria," Lisa told Walter. "I grabbed some when I got your coffee."

"Crackers?" He looked up from his computer as she set his mug down.

"I guess she has a bunch of soup but no crackers," Lisa said. "I called her before I went downstairs to see if she wanted anything to eat, but that's all she wants. I'm going to run it over to her."

"Okay. Hope her stomach feels better." Walter turned back to his computer.

Lisa strolled over to the other side of the building, swinging a little bag. She knocked on the door to Tina's apartment and entered.

"Hey, your delivery is here. Crackers to go," she called.

Tina came out of the bedroom. Her cheeks were slightly flushed.

"Thanks." She took the bag, pulled out a cracker and devoured it.

"Where's your soup?" Lisa asked.

"I haven't warmed it up yet."

"I'll do it for you." Lisa went into the kitchen and took a can from the cabinet. "You look like you might have a fever. How do you feel?" She emptied the soup into a pot and set it on the burner.

"I'm okay. Just a little tired. I'm going to go to the store tomorrow before work. I have to pick up some stuff that Gerta recommended."

Lisa came out of the kitchen. "What stuff?"

"Just vitamins and stuff."

Lisa sat on the couch beside her. "You've got me worried. You don't look good. What did she say?"

"Well..." Tina struggled. She so wanted to tell Lisa.

"It's the beginning of an ulcer. I knew it." Lisa shook her head.

"I know I let stress get to me. Everybody's right, but it's not an ulcer."

"Is it something worse? You're scaring me. What did she say? You can tell me."

"I promised myself I wouldn't tell anyone else until I took the test."

"What test? A colonoscopy?" Lisa guessed. "Wait. Who did you tell before me?"

"I talked to George on the phone."

"Okay."

Tina reached into the bag for another cracker.

"Did you schedule the test yet? What kind of test is it, anyway?" Lisa asked. "Do you want me to go to the store for you? I can go right now. What do you need?"

"That would be great," Tina said. "Gerta's list is on the counter."

"What's this test you have to do? Do you want me to go with you?"

Tina tried to suppress a smile.

"Why are you looking at me like that?" Lisa wrinkled her brow.

"I'll give you my credit card," Tina said. "I want you to buy something else for me."

"Why are you being so weird and mysterious? Tell me right now," Lisa demanded.

"I want you to buy me a pregnancy test." Tina drew in her breath, waiting for a reaction.

"What?" Lisa shrieked. "That's what's wrong with you? This is huge."

"I know," Tina said. "I'm almost positive. Gerta told me, but I promised George I'd do a test."

"I'm going to be an aunt," Lisa squealed. "Kind of."

***

Skyler Rose turned around when Nick entered the dressing room. Her high-heeled boots made her appear even taller. Long blonde hair hung down her back and her clothing was boho chic. Sunglasses sat atop her head and bracelets jangled on her wrist, while rings adorned almost every finger, including her thumbs.

"Nick." Her teeth were dazzling white when she smiled at him. "Great show."

"Thanks."

He was a bit stunned to see someone like her backstage. He hadn't met many celebrities yet, other than Isabella and Lilliana.

"Oh." She looked past him at Isabella lingering in the doorway. "Hi. We met at an awards show. Don't ask me which one. They're all the same." She laughed lightly.

"I remember," Isabella responded.

"I probably already told you this, but I'm a big fan," she said to Isabella.

"Thanks. You have a great voice," Isabella

responded.

Skyler waved her hand. "I'm actually trying to get into acting now." She turned to Nick. "Can we go get a drink or something?"

"Right." He glanced at Isabella as they swept past her.

"Nice to see you." Skyler smiled back at her.

"Can I go?" Kris called after them.

"No," Nick said over his shoulder.

He followed Skyler to a waiting car behind the venue. He wasn't sure what she wanted with him. She didn't look like the kind who was up for a revolution. She instructed the driver, and they were off.

"I hope I didn't get you in trouble with Isabella," she said.

"We're just friends."

"That's what I thought." Skyler pressed a button, and a partition went up, separating the back seat from the driver. "Well, Nick Claus."

He looked at her with surprise. "Who told you that?"

"You don't have to pretend with me. I talked to your sister on the phone. That reporter who did the article about her gave you up because I want to option your sister's story for a movie," Skyler explained. "I think I'd be perfect in the role. What do you think? Would I look good with white hair?"

He shrugged. "That's Tina's thing. I'm not into it."

"I know. I just wanted to meet you." Skyler studied him. "I want you to tell me everything, Nick."

"Everything?" He narrowed his eyes.

"I went up there, but your sister wasn't around. I want you to tell me what it's like growing up with Santa as your father. What's it really like? You can tell me."

"Nothing to tell." Nick leaned back into the soft seat.

She crossed her long legs. "You're my prisoner tonight, Nick, and I'm not letting you go until you give me what I want." She giggled.

"Right."

"Am I scaring you?"

Nick shook his head.

"I never could play a good villain." Skyler pouted. "Just tell me about your sister so I can play her."

"What's with the way you talk?" he asked.

"I'm from England."

"The Beatles are from there."

"That's right. You like the Beatles?" she asked.

"They're only the greatest band ever."

"You think so?"

"*Black Ice* is a lot like them. It's like syn... syn... fate."

"Synchronicity? But your music is so different."

"It transcends that. It's like destiny or karma or something. We have band members named George and John, and George is a vegetarian and we got discovered by a brilliant manager. Coincidences like that," he said, peering out the window. He couldn't tell where they were.

"We're just going to my hotel," Skyler said. "We can have drinks in my room. I hate going out. I always get mobbed."

"Right."

"Then I want you to tell me about growing up at the North Pole and being Santa's son and all about your sister."

A scowl darkened Nick's face. When was his childhood going to let go of him? His family name gnawed at him like one of those carnivorous plants. He'd seen one in a movie recently. It was pretty whacked, but at least it wasn't set at the North Pole. He just couldn't seem to get far enough away from it.

***

The instructions had advised doing the test in the morning. After a sleepless night, Tina sat staring at the results. With trembling hands, she picked up her phone and texted George.

"Call your parents."

She'd send him a follow-up email when she got to her office, in case he didn't get the text. Then he could call her if he was available to talk.

"What did it say?" Lisa screamed, running toward her in the hall as Tina neared her office.

Tina laughed and nodded.

"Congratulations, Tina." Walter came over and hugged her.

"I didn't tell him," Lisa said quickly. "He figured it out because of the crackers."

"My ex-wife had to keep crackers with her all the time. Otherwise, she'd get sick to her stomach," he said. "It hit me last night."

"Have you told your parents yet?" Lisa asked.

"Not yet. I'm going to call them right now." Tina turned on her computer.

"How do you feel?" Walter asked. "Any time you need to rest, just let us know."

"Thanks, Walter. I feel fine right now. That ginger tea really helps and I have crackers with me." She patted her purse.

"Did you take your vitamins?" Lisa asked.

"Yes." Tina smiled. Her stomach still bubbled, but now it was with excitement.

"Let's go so she can call her parents." Walter pulled Lisa's arm.

Tina picked up the telephone receiver on her desk and inhaled a deep breath. She dialed and listened to it ring.

"Oh, Tina. I was just going to call you," Clara said. "Melatonin."

"What?"

"That's what Gerta told your father to take to help him sleep. It was driving me crazy that I couldn't remember it, but it came to me and I wrote it down so I could tell you."

"Okay," Tina said.

"I was researching stomach pain online and…"

"Mom, I wanted to tell you what Gerta said."

"You went to see her? Good. What did she say? You should listen to her. I can't remember her ever being wrong. When I was pregnant with you, she told me you were going to be a girl, but your father was sure I was going to have a boy."

"Pregnant."

"Yes, when I was pregnant with you."

"Pregnant." Tina couldn't seem to utter anything else.

"Yes. When I was pregnant with you," Clara repeated. "Are you okay?"

"Mom." Tina took another deep breath. "I'm pregnant."

Clara gasped. "Goodness! Why didn't I figure that out? Where's your father? Dear?"

"Gerta told me, but I also took a pregnancy test this morning."

"I can't believe it. This is the best news. Oh my goodness, Tina! Were you able to reach George yet? I know they're on tour somewhere."

"Yes. I told him last night," Tina said.

"Last night? Why didn't you call me sooner?"

"I wanted to take the test first, to be sure."

"Oh, there he is in the kitchen. What are you eating, dear? We just ate."

"Mom, tell him," Tina said impatiently.

"Yes, it's Tina on the phone. She's pregnant! Isn't that wonderful news? Oh, my goodness." Clara gasped again. "We're going to be grandparents."

Tina laughed at her mother's excitement.

"When are you due?" Clara asked.

"The beginning of January."

The realization suddenly hit Tina. She'd have to do the delivery on Christmas Eve when she was quite pregnant. It had never been done, but she'd already broken lots of gender barriers. Besides, many women worked right up to their due dates. And she could too. She patted her tummy. Baby on board the sleigh.

21 *Feeding the Machine*

"Do you really believe all that stuff, or is it just your image?" Skyler shifted toward him on the plush couch in her suite. She held a glass of wine.

Nick took a gulp of beer from the bottle in his grasp. He could see the glittering night sky out the window behind her. It was an impressive view.

"The corporatocracy is brainwashing the masses to become consumers feeding the machine of capitalism," he stated.

"Where do you get this stuff?" She shook her head. "And what does it have to do with Christmas?"

"Christmas is about greed. And judgment. Teaching kids to believe in the Naughty or Nice reward system," he expounded.

"But our careers depend on sales," she reasoned. "I mean, let's face it. We're pushing ourselves as products by selling songs and tickets to concerts."

"The system is set up that way, but I can still get my message out there and wake people up."

"But don't you think we're feeding the machine by participating?"

"It's a monster," Nick said. "It's going to get fed no matter what we do until we change things."

"I thought you said it was a machine." Skyler poured herself more wine.

"It's... both." He shrugged.

"I'm really surprised to hear you slam Christmas, Nick. I mean, you *know* the North Pole is real and not some fantasy."

"That makes it all the more insidjurous... insidientary... insid..."

"Insidious?"

"I knew you'd get it." He waved his beer bottle. "My father wanted me to take over and play Santa, but I wouldn't do it. I couldn't perpetuate that materialistic, fake holiday."

"Not many people would pass up the chance to be Santa," Skyler said with admiration. "I don't even want to pass up the opportunity to *play* Santa... Santina in a movie."

"You're too talented to waste your time on a kid's movie," he snorted.

Skyler wrinkled her brow. "Yeah? Maybe you're right."

Nick plucked another bottle out of the six-pack on the glass coffee table.

"So what do you think we should do, then? Be out on the streets protesting?" she asked.

"The masses need to mobilize and have a revolution."

"I don't know if that would accomplish anything." Skyler sipped her wine. "I think we need to change things from the inside by voting in the right people. That's the only way to make lasting changes in any country."

"That sounds nice and all but people get, like, corrupted when they get caught in the political machine. It's all a big game, anyway. The real people running things are not the figureheads we elect."

"Ah, there's a vast conspiracy to rule the world." She nodded.

"The people we elect are just like corporate puppets controlled by the real dictators who run the world. They keep us distracted with smoke and windows."

"You mean smoke and mirrors." Skyler stretched her legs onto the coffee table. "You have a very dark view of the world."

"Smoke and mirrors," Nick repeated thoughtfully. "I'll have to write a song with that title."

"I should go after more serious roles," she stated.

"You could play someone who uncovers the truth and saves the world or something," Nick said. "You could be a scientist who invents like a truth serum and makes all the politicians tell the truth."

"A scientist. I like the sound of that. I could play a

scientist who figures out how to reverse climate change and saves the world from a giant storm."

"Mother Earth is taking it back. We've disrespected her, and she's pissed off."

Skyler laughed heartily. "You're a trip, Nick." She set her wineglass down and inched closer. "I don't disagree with you, but don't you think the earth runs in natural cycles?"

"We should tread lightly when we're on the ground," he intoned.

"I think it's 'tread lightly on the earth.'" Skyler giggled. "Your sister isn't anything like you, is she?"

"Tina believes in the family business. It's her thing, and that's cool. I'm an artist."

"Me too." Skyler tilted her head. "You're right. It's different from being a celebrity. I should focus on things I want to do, not just on making money." She absentmindedly turned the ring on her thumb.

"Right."

Skyler scanned the room. "The problem is... I like all this stuff." She waved her hand. "I like room service and nice things and traveling and my big beautiful house." She sighed. "What can you do?"

***

"I called my parents," George told Tina.

She swiveled in her desk chair. "I told mine too."

"My mother wants to know your due date."

"I'm not exactly sure. Sometime in early January."

"But won't that interfere... What about Christmas Eve?"

"You'll be up here and so will my parents and Gerta will be right here to deliver it," she said. "Women work right up till..." Her voice trailed off.

"Okay," he said slowly.

"What did your parents say?" Tina changed the subject.

"They're thrilled. Evan's in school now and they

can't wait to have another little one in the family. I don't know whether Gemma will ever have kids. Guess it's up to the boys in the family."

"Do you think Garrett and Tonia will have another one?"

"I don't know. He's a chef and Tonia's a teacher. They both have busy careers, so they might not."

"You don't think Gemma wants kids?" Tina asked.

"I wouldn't be surprised if she doesn't have any. She likes her freedom."

"What about Loren?"

"You heard her. She always says it's not serious," he said. "Although Loren seems to think it is."

"Ironic, huh?"

"I know. He was the one who didn't want to be tied down," George said.

"Yes. He even saw Lisa for a little while."

"Then he went after Isabella. That was probably just to get at Nick, though."

"Oh, I have to call Nick and tell him the news," Tina remembered.

"I can tell him unless you'd rather do it. I don't know where he is right now," George said. "Kris told me that Skyler Rose came backstage to meet him and they left."

"Wait. Nick is with Skyler Rose?"

"Yeah. She was at the show and came backstage."

"This can't be a coincidence."

"What do you mean?"

"She's the one who wants to option the article about me for a movie."

"Do you think she knows who Nick is, and that's why she's hanging out with him?" he asked.

"That's what I'm wondering."

"But Nick can't give her permission to do the movie. Wouldn't that have to come from Jill or the magazine?"

"Yes, but maybe she's trying to get information on us or our family for the movie."

"Whatever it is, don't let it get to you. It doesn't matter. She'll do the movie or she won't and it has nothing to do with us right now. We have something more important to think about."

Tina smiled. "You're right. I'm not going to worry about it."

"Don't worry about anything. You have Walter and Lisa up there to help you with work and you have Gerta to help you with your health," he said. "And I'll be up there soon."

"Not soon enough."

"I know. Not for another few months," he said. "I hope you can come to our show in L.A. but not unless you're up to it."

"Okay. I miss you," Tina said forlornly.

"I miss you too, wife," George responded.

***

Nick had fallen asleep on the large couch. It was more comfortable than the bed in his hotel room. He squinted at the daylight pouring through the wide window framed by the heavy drapes they'd never closed.

"I hope I didn't make too much noise and wake you up."

Skyler wore a white terrycloth robe, and her hair hung in wet strands down her back.

He pushed himself up. "Uh..."

"You fell asleep last night," she said. "The shower's free if you want it."

"I should get back," he said groggily.

"I ordered breakfast for us. I'll have my driver take you back after we eat."

He rubbed his eyes with his fists.

"I fell asleep on the couch too," she confessed. "I woke up early in the morning and got into the bed in the other room."

Nick yawned.

Skyler sat down beside him. "Nick." Her eyes were bright with excitement. "I've been thinking about it since I woke up."

"What? Where's the bathroom?"

She pointed, and he got up to use it.

"What?" he asked again when he returned.

"Our conversation really got me thinking."

"Right."

"No, really." She indicated the phone on the side table. "Do you need to call someone and let them know where you are?"

"Yeah." Nick pulled his cell phone out of his pocket and texted George. "At a hotel with Skyler. Back soon."

"Everybody I talk to just goes on about sales and numbers or how much their next project will bring in." She grinned at him. "But you don't give a fig about any of that."

He shrugged.

"It's not all about that, is it?"

"I'm an artist."

"When did I lose sight of that?" she wondered. "You've opened my eyes, Nick."

He closed his eyes and yawned again.

"There's so much going on in the world that's more important. What we do is trivial."

"Right."

"I know your songs have messages, but think what we could do together."

"What?" Nick wasn't sure where she was going with this train of thought, and even less sure he was ready to board.

There was a knock on the door.

"Room service," Skyler squealed and jumped up to let them in.

A young man rolled a cart into the room and Skyler shooed him away after giving him a generous tip. She pushed the cart over to a small table by the window and gestured for Nick to join her.

"I'm famished. The food is fantastic here." She seated herself and dug in.

The tray was filled with a plethora of breakfast items hidden beneath covered platters. Skyler had ordered pancakes and eggs and strawberries with cream, French toast and waffles and flaky biscuits, coffee and tea and juice.

"This is a lot of food," Nick observed.

Skyler shrugged. "I wasn't sure what you wanted. You look like you burn a lot of energy on stage. You probably consume a lot of calories when you're on tour."

"Right." He guzzled orange juice.

Skyler watched as he piled a little of everything onto his plate.

"I knew it." She laughed.

"Don't want to waste it," he muttered.

"What did you eat growing up?"

"The typical diet, I guess. Then my mother became vegetarian and lost weight and we all eat healthier now when we have family dinners."

"Really?" she asked with interest. "What about milk and cookies for Santa?"

"Not anymore."

They ate silently for a few minutes. The sun was shining brightly on the day outside. Nick thought about the show ahead that night. Isabella was warming up to him again. He wanted to resume their last conversation that Skyler had interrupted. It finally felt as if Isabella's stubborn defenses were weakening and she was about to recognize her true feelings for him. No time to waste. The end of the tour was drawing closer.

"What are you thinking about?" Skyler pulled him back to reality.

"The show tonight."

"I have a really great idea."

"What?"

"I think you should come to my house in L.A. after the tour and we can do this together." Skyler had a little smile on her face.

"Do what?" What was she talking about?

"We can write the screenplay together."

"What screenplay?"

"The one you pitched me last night. The one about

the scientist," she reminded him. "But we can make it two scientists, and maybe they're rivals or something. One is working on a truth serum that she'll get a politician to take and the other scientist is trying to figure out how to slow climate change and avert this big impending storm."

Nick looked at her blankly.

"The one we talked about last night. It's brilliant," she gushed.

"Twins," he said.

"What about twins?"

"The scientists could be twin sisters. Then you could play both." He poured maple syrup on his French toast.

"Nick!" Skyler screamed. "I love it!"

22 *Storm Warning*

Tina had called a meeting of all the department leads. Elves, tall and small, had assembled and were standing around chatting when Tina entered the large meeting room with Lisa and Walter.

"It's good to be back," Tina said when everyone had settled in their seats. Smiling faces met her own. This group truly felt like family to her. "I hope all of you had an enjoyable break."

"I was ready to get back to work," someone said.

"My kids were driving me crazy," a female elf added, and everyone laughed.

Tina smiled. "I know we usually have our first meeting much sooner, but I had a personal health issue..."

"Tell them." Lisa nudged her.

"My news is that I'm pregnant and I've had terrible morning sickness..."

Congratulations were enthusiastically called out, and some elves clapped.

Tina blushed. "Thank you."

"Morning sickness is the worst," a female elf said. "But it usually goes away in a few months."

Tina nodded. "Lots of crackers and ginger tea for now."

"Let us know if you need anything," someone said.

"Thank you." Tina folded her hands on the table. "Okay, back to business. Everything went really well last year. We haven't had to hire any new employees because we've become so much more efficient with the improvements to the machinery and the departments doing such a good job working together."

"How's the old man?"

"Santa's fine," Tina answered. "He and my mother will be up for the Northern Lights Festival again."

"What about Nick? He hasn't been up here for years."

"I know. He's been busy with his band," Tina said.

"*Black Ice* should play for the festival!"

"Unfortunately, that's not possible because the band members don't know who we are," she answered. "Except for my husband, of course."

"Let's get back to business," Walter said, rescuing her.

"Yes," Tina agreed with relief.

They went around the table for updates on each department. Some leads also shared news about their families or time off.

"We're still having trouble with that one chute in the mailroom," said Rusty, a red-haired elf.

"The same one as last year?" Tina asked. "I thought we fixed it."

"I did too, but it's catching again."

"Ken." Tina turned to one of the taller elves who was head of the IT department. "I think we need the help of an engineer this time. Maybe Jamie can modify it or design a fix for us."

"She's still on her honeymoon with Amy. I think they'll be back next week," he said. "Tuesday or Wednesday."

"They've been gone a long time. Are you sure they're coming back?" Tina asked.

"Yeah. Amy had a family thing," he said. "Her aunt is in the hospital."

"Oh. Then tell them to take all the time they need. The chute can wait a little longer," Tina said.

"I'll look at it and see what I can do in the meantime," Rusty offered.

"Okay. Keep me updated." She looked at every face gathered around the table. "Does anybody have anything else?"

Lisa raised her hand.

Tina nodded at her.

"If anybody wants to help decorate for the festival this year, just let me know," Lisa said. "I could use some new ideas."

"Lisa's been doing an outstanding job for the past few years," Tina acknowledged.

A light round of applause broke out, and then more elves spoke up.

"It's been cold in the toy shop."

"The elevator's making a funny noise."

"Can we get pumpkin pie in the cafeteria?"

Tina glanced at Lisa, who was writing everything down.

"Have you seen the reindeer yet?" Rusty asked. "I saw them down at the pub and Blitzen..." He shook his head.

"What?" Lisa asked.

"He said something about a big storm this year."

Tina and Lisa looked at each other.

"I haven't been out to the barn yet," Tina answered. "I'll look into it. Thanks, everyone. If there's nothing else, let's get back to work."

There was the sounds of chairs scraping back and the pattering of footsteps as everyone filed out.

"Have you heard anything about a storm?" Tina asked Walter.

He shook his head. "But you know the reindeer can sense things like that."

"I'm going out there right now," Tina said.

"Ooh, can I go too?" Lisa asked.

"Okay." Tina pushed back her chair. "I'll go to the apartment and get my coat and boots."

"I'll meet you there." Lisa rose from her seat.

"I'll hold down the fort," Walter said.

***

Nick was at sound check. His head was throbbing slightly from the night before. It was probably more from lack of sleep than from the beer.

"You and Skyler?" George asked, adjusting his guitar strap. "She doesn't seem like your type."

Nick shook his head. "It's not like that."

"Sure," Milo said, punching his shoulder as he walked by. "I'm proud of you." He climbed up onto the drum platform.

George stepped closer to Nick. "You know she wants to do a movie about Tina, right?" he asked in a hushed tone.

"Hey, share the details!" Milo shouted.

Nick attempted to adjust the mic higher on the stand. "She's over that. We're doing a movie about twin scientists."

"We?" George twisted the ring on the stand and pulled up the mic.

"What are we doing?" Kris bounded over like an eager puppy.

Nick ignored him. "After the tour," he said to George.

"What about after the tour?" George asked.

"She wants me to come to L.A. and help her write this movie." He took a bottle of water from Kris and gulped it down. "Man, I'm thirsty."

"She wants you to help her write a screenplay?" George asked incredulously.

"Why not? The story is my idea," Nick said. "You're going to go visit Tina and the other guys are taking a break, so why not?"

"What about me?" Kris asked.

Nick looked at him and shrugged. "Visit your parents."

"Then they'll want me to run the Kringle Café again," he wailed.

"The what café?" John asked.

"Hey, I have an announcement," George called out to distract him.

"What's up?" Milo asked.

"Tina's pregnant." George beamed. He had meant to tell Nick first, but this had happened.

Nick stared at him for a moment. "You knocked up my sister?"

Milo let out a guffaw.

"You're going to be an uncle." George patted Nick's shoulder.

"I'm just messing with you." Nick hugged him. "Congrats, man."

"I'm going to be an uncle, too." Kris hugged them both.

"You won't be an uncle," George said as they disengaged. "You'll be a second cousin, I think."

"Can't the kid call me Uncle Kris?"

"Yeah. That's fine," George said.

"Tell us about Skyler," Kris prodded Nick. "She's hot."

"Yeah, tell us about Skyler," Milo teased.

"I'd like to hear about Skyler."

Everyone turned to see Isabella standing by a side door with her arms folded.

"Uh oh," Milo muttered.

"Congratulations, George." She smiled warmly at him.

"Thanks, Isabella." George busied himself with his guitar. He pushed Nick. "Go talk to her."

Nick crossed the stage and tripped as Isabella disappeared out the door.

"Go make the peace," John advised. "You're singing with her tonight."

***

The barn door was closed, which was unusual. It was most often ajar. Tina and Lisa shivered outside while Tina knocked on the door with a gloved hand.

"Nobody can hear that." Lisa's voice was muffled by the scarf wrapped around her neck and lower face.

She kicked the large wooden door. They both kicked and then waited. The door abruptly creaked open.

"How long have you been out here, girls?" Dancer asked. "Come in before you freeze."

They hurried inside over to the wood stove and held out their hands toward the warmth.

"It's so wonderful to see you," Dancer loped over.

"You too," Tina answered with chattering teeth.

"I'll let everyone know you're here," she said and ambled toward the back of the barn.

"Tina! Lisa!" Rudolph dashed out.

"How are rehearsals for your play going?" Lisa asked.

Rudolph dug his hoof into the packed dirt floor. "I really wanted to do a musical, but everyone voted against it. Don't you think it would've been merry fun?"

"Not everyone can sing as well as you," Tina consoled him.

He looked up brightly. "You're right! Maybe that's why no one else wanted to do it. That makes sense."

The rest of the reindeer trotted out except for Blitzen and Donner who strolled together.

"I'm the director," Blitzen was saying. "I don't want a dance number. It would be out of context."

"But I never get the chance to use my tap dancing skills," Donner protested. "Pretty soon I'll forget how."

Blitzen let out a sigh. "Now I know why directors have no hair. They pull it all out."

"Hi, Blitzen," Lisa called.

"Lisa," he said. "Welcome back, Tina."

"I have news," Tina announced.

"Is it good news?" Rudolph asked.

"It's great news." Tina smiled, rubbing her hands together before the wood stove. "I'm pregnant."

"That's wonderful!" Dancer said.

There were murmurs of congratulations.

"When are you due?" Prancer asked.

Tina's smile disappeared. "Around the beginning of January."

The reindeer glanced at each other.

"But, Tina, that's so close..." Vixen said.

"I can still do the delivery on Christmas Eve," Tina asserted.

Everyone looked at Blitzen. He shook his enormous head. "I don't know. We never had to worry about this with Santa."

"It'll be fine," Tina said. "As long as Gerta says it's okay."

"Gerta will know," Cupid stated with a nod.

"If that big storm doesn't hit first," Comet added.

"Rusty told us you mentioned something about a storm." Tina raised her eyebrows at Blitzen.

Concern filled his big brown eyes. "That's right. Every fifty years or so, we get a major storm here and we're overdue."

"So it might not happen this year." Lisa waved her mittened hand dismissively.

"Oh, it's happening this year," Blitzen proclaimed. "It's definitely coming this year."

"It is? When?" Tina asked.

"Not sure. Later this year."

"How big a storm is this?" Lisa asked, wide-eyed.

"The last storm was about eighty years ago. Snowdrifts buried half the houses in the village. The wind tore down the original barn and ripped part of the roof off the warehouse," Blitzen recalled.

"I thought a fire burned down the warehouse," Tina said.

"Yes. A lantern broke and burned most of it down," Blitzen said. "That's where the original toy shop was, and it was rebuilt into a warehouse. We were expanding, anyway, but it was a terrible year. It took a long time to recover."

"There must be a way to reinforce the buildings," Lisa said.

"They made the buildings sturdier," Blitzen said. "Now they'll be put to the test."

Tina had a horrible feeling of dread. She put her hand on her tummy. Christmas Eve, the storm, the baby—all seemed to be converging.

23 *Mothers*

"Hello, Gloria," Clara said. She put her hand over the phone. "It's George's mother," she said to Santa.

He raised his eyebrows and continued eating his veggie wrap. A bit of lettuce fell onto his plate.

"Have you heard the news?" Gloria asked.

"Yes. We heard. Isn't it wonderful?"

"Garrett's little boy, Evan, started school last year, and I was just saying to Grover that it would be nice when George and Tina started a family."

"Yes, we're so excited. It'll be the first grandchild for us," Clara said. "Though I thought they'd wait a little longer."

"We did too." Gloria laughed. "I'm just thrilled. George's grandmother has already started crocheting a baby blanket. She made one for Evan."

"Goodness. I'm going to be a grandmother." Clara fanned herself with her hand. "Don't you feel too young, Gloria?"

"Yes, I do. My grandmother seemed so old when I was a kid, but here G.G. is going to be a great-grandmother again and she doesn't seem so old, does she?" Gloria asked.

"Not at all."

"Do you know where Tina will have the baby? Is she going to come down to Florida so you can help her?" Gloria asked.

"She has a midwife up north," Clara said. "We're going up for the holidays and we'll stay there for the baby."

"Well, we might have to come up to see the little one then," Gloria said.

"No, no. Don't worry about that. Tina always comes back down to Florida once the holiday season is over," Clara said.

"That's right. Your toy business is seasonal."

"Yes, I'm sure they'll stop in Boston on their way

down here," Clara said.

"That would work out great," Gloria enthused. "I wonder how Evan will react to his new little cousin."

"How fun," Clara said. "How is everyone there?"

"We're all fine. Tonia is finishing up the school year, and then we'll have more time with Evan during summer vacation. Garrett is training another chef and we haven't seen much of Gemma. I think she's working on another book."

"I really should read one of her books."

"And how's Nick? George said the tour is going well," Gloria said.

"That's what we hear. It really is amazing how popular their band has become."

"Now don't tell George, but that's not our type of music. We prefer real rock-n-roll." Gloria laughed.

"I hear you," Clara said. She glanced over in time to see Santa spill water on the table. "I'll get that, dear."

"Is everything all right?" Gloria asked.

"Yes, Nicholas just knocked over his glass."

"I'll let you go then, Clara. Good talking to you. Congratulations to us!"

"Yes. Okay." Clara hung up the phone.

Santa had gone into the kitchen for a towel. He threw it over the spreading puddle of water.

"Let me get a washcloth." Clara hurried into the kitchen and grabbed it off the edge of the sink. She patted the underside of his plate and he took it with him and settled into his chair.

"I'm a little worried," she said, mopping up the water.

"Hmm." Santa looked at her as he took a bite. "We need a little more sauce or whatever you put in these wraps next time."

"Okay."

Clara went into the kitchen and wrung out the washcloth and towel over the sink. She took a dry towel from the drawer and returned to the table. She stood holding it.

"What did you say before?" Santa finished his wrap and set his plate on the tray beside his chair. He plucked a piece of loose lettuce off his plate and popped it into his mouth.

"I'm worried about Tina."

"She's fine. She's just pregnant."

"But she's due right after Christmas. It might not be safe for her to do the delivery. Don't you think it'll be too much for her riding around in the sleigh all night?" Clara twisted the towel in her hands.

Santa wrinkled his brow. "I don't know. I haven't thought about it."

Clara sank down into a chair. "Gerta will know. Tina will have to talk to her about it. She's just so adamant about doing it."

"She'll listen to Gerta." Santa picked up the remote.

"I hope so." Clara threw the towel over the remaining beads of moisture on the table.

That Christmas Eve sleigh ride might not be good for the baby. Or Tina. That night took so much out of her. This was very worrisome.

***

Nick meandered backstage, searching for Isabella. She had no right to be angry at him after she'd made it crystal clear that she wasn't interested in more than a friendship with him. But still. Her defenses had cracked, and she was on the verge of finally acknowledging her feelings for him. Why was she being so stubborn about it?

Skyler had appeared out of the blue and offered him an exciting opportunity. He had no interest in writing a screenplay, but he could write the music. An epic rock opera would reach a whole new audience with his message of revolution. It could become a whole movement. That would be totally stellar.

"Nick." Isabella approached him. "Are you looking for me?"

"Right." He tried to gather and focus his thoughts.

"Well?" She folded her arms and narrowed her eyes.

He stared at her. Her stance and expression reminded him of someone.

"Your mother..." he said.

"My mother?" Her eyes widened. "Why are you bringing her up?"

"She's wrong," he said. "You're a hella artist and singer."

Isabella's angry expression dissolved into a tentative smile. "Really?"

"Your mother is an energy sucker. You know, like some people do that. They get off on bringing you down."

This wasn't what Nick had planned to say. The words had simply tumbled from his mouth.

Isabella nodded. "You're exactly right."

Nick nodded along with her.

"Hey," she said suddenly. "You and Skyler? Is that true? I didn't think she was your type, but..."

"She's not." He scowled and shook his head.

"But you were gone all night, and I thought..." She put up her hand. "Never mind. It's none of my business."

"Right." Nick furrowed his brow, trying to think of the right thing to say. "I fell asleep on the couch."

"Oh." Isabella smiled. "It's really none of my business who you..."

"Skyler wants me to help her write a movie, but I was thinking I could do the music. I could, like, spread my branches and..." he rambled.

"Branch out? Why does she want you to write a screenplay with her? You're a musician."

Nick shrugged. "We started talking, and I told her she should play a scientist and she liked my idea."

Isabella nodded slowly. "And you want to write the score? Smart move. You could probably do it. So, this is about business, then?"

"Right."

"Good." Isabella touched his arm. "I knew that

glossy plastic celebrity type wasn't your thing."

"Not," he snorted.

They shared a laugh.

"She wants me to go to her place in L.A. after the tour and work on the movie with her," Nick shared.

Isabella pulled her hand away. "Are you serious? Why did I believe you?"

Nick stared at her blankly.

"You like her," she accused. "Or maybe you just like the publicity like when you pretended we were together."

"That was your idea," he reminded her.

"You want to be linked with her." Isabella pointed a finger at him. "I knew it. Admit it!"

Nick shook his head as she stalked off. What had just happened? She was so unpredictable.

"Ooh, you're in trouble," Kris said gleefully.

Nick hadn't seen him lurking in the shadows backstage.

"Get lost, Kris."

"You don't need her. You have Skyler."

"That's just business."

"Sure it is," Kris said, attempting to wink but blinking both eyes. "That's not what Isabella thinks. Girls know these things with their inter.... inta... Man, is she jealous."

Jealous? Nick hadn't thought of that possibility, but that had to be it. She was insanely jealous of Skyler because she thought they were into each other. But now that he knew, how could he get her to realize it and express her feelings for him?

***

"Are you taking the vitamins and supplements I recommended?" Gerta asked.

"Yes." Tina blew on the steaming hot chocolate in her mug. She dropped a few mini marshmallows into the steaming liquid and watched them melt into white foam. "When will I start to show?"

"You will be showing by the time everyone comes for the festival." Gerta smiled.

Tina put her hand on her tummy. "I can't wait to get over this all-day morning sickness."

"Just remember to keep something in your stomach and drink the ginger tea," Gerta said. "You are almost finished with your first trimester and then it will go away. Keep eating nutritious foods and you will have a healthy baby."

"Yes, I will." Tina warmed her hands on her mug. "How are *you*, Gerta?"

"We are all fine. I have been helping Sonia with the wedding plans. There is so much to do."

"I can't believe I've been married for over a year now." Tina shook her head. "But we've spent so much of it apart, I don't know how I got pregnant. I mean..." She blushed.

"Yes." Gerta pushed a plate of cinnamon muffins toward her. "Your parents must be excited. And your in-laws."

"Yes, they're ecstatic. George's brother has a little boy who's five now, and I think his parents are ready for another baby in the family."

"This child will continue your family tradition, yes?"

"If it's a girl." Tina wrinkled her brow. "I guess it could go either way."

"There is plenty of time to think about it."

"Yes. And we'll probably have more than one. I don't know. George and I have never really talked about it."

"You and George will have more than one." Gerta nodded.

Tina was reaching for a muffin and her hand stopped. "We will?"

"I can say no more."

Tina set her muffin on a napkin and tore off a piece. The scent of cinnamon rushed up to her nose. More than one child. She and George would make a family together. What a joyful thought.

"I want you to come by once a month until we get closer to your delivery." Gerta smiled. "I mean delivering the baby, of course."

Tina smiled.

"You can have an ultrasound at the hospital and any other tests that are necessary, and one of the doctors can do an exam," Gerta explained.

"Okay, but I prefer this," Tina said. "Sitting at your table eating a muffin and drinking hot chocolate."

"Yes. I do as well."

"Oh, I wanted to ask you about something that Blitzen said." Tina remembered.

Gerta took a sip from her mug.

"He said something about a big storm this year. I'm a little worried about it."

"Yes. I am afraid it is true. It is coming before the new year," she said solemnly.

"How bad will it be?" Tina bit her lip.

"The last storm eighty years ago was very bad. Now our buildings can withstand more force, but we must not take this lightly," Gerta warned. "I may know more as it gets closer. It will be a powerful storm. We must prepare."

24 *Rowdy Reindeer*

"Start growing your beard. We're going up early," Clara told Santa as she perused flights on her laptop.

"Why? That apartment is too small for all of us," Santa grumbled. "We shouldn't stay any longer than necessary."

"Our baby is having a baby," Clara squealed. "I can't wait to see her. She's going to need our help."

"Geez." Santa stuck his little finger in his ear and wiggled it.

"I have to talk to Gerta about how Tina is doing." Clara whirled and pointed a finger at him. "And we're not leaving until that baby is born. I'm not going to miss it. I don't care how long it hangs on."

"Isn't it due at the beginning of January?" He frowned.

"Yes, but remember I was late with both the kids by a few weeks," she reminded him.

Santa groaned. "Tina always comes back here before New Year's. Why can't she have the baby here?"

"She wants Gerta to deliver the baby. We're going to have to stay up there until it happens."

"Isn't George going to be there too?"

"Of course. He's the father."

"She doesn't need us, then. We'll see the baby when she comes back here in January."

"I'm her mother. I have to be there," Clara declared. "She needs me."

Santa shook his head.

"I can't wait to put my hand on Tina's tummy and feel that baby kick. I hope she doesn't have trouble like I did with Nick."

"Nick has been a problem since before he was born." Santa rolled his eyes.

"That's true. My morning sickness was worse, and the birth was more difficult because he was bigger than Tina."

"He used to cry all the time," Santa recalled. "He drove me crazy."

"Nick always needed more attention right from the start," Clara agreed. "Tina was easy."

"And she was always more interested in the toy shop. I don't know why I never noticed."

"You were too busy trying to get Nick interested."

"Because he was supposed to be the next Santa," he said defensively. "How was I supposed to know that our daughter could do it? The job was always passed from father to son."

"Nobody's blaming you, dear. I didn't know either." Clara squinted at her computer screen.

"When is George going up?"

"Probably right after the tour ends."

"Let him go up first," Santa said.

"That's a good idea." Clara nodded. "We should give them some time. We'll go up a few weeks after."

Santa rubbed his chin. "Guess I'll keep shaving for now."

***

Tina was checking flights at the same time as Clara. Her morning sickness was subsiding, and she felt well enough to travel. She couldn't wait to see George in L.A. She wondered if she should surprise him. She could have Nick pick her up at the airport. No. It would be too hard to keep it to herself when she talked with George on the phone. She was too excited at the thought of seeing him.

She found a flight and sent him a quick email before she confirmed. It was easier to reach him this way when they were on tour. An email popped in from her mother asking when George would arrive at the North Pole. They wanted to come up early. She checked her calendar. The Northern Lights Festival was in September. George planned to fly up in late August. The band had some smaller gigs set up, but he could miss them. If he stayed until the birth, that would give them months together. Of course, her parents would be there for most of that time as well. That wouldn't give them much privacy. Not ideal, but that was okay. She wanted them there for the birth too.

Lisa came into her office and placed a steaming mug of ginger tea on her desk.

"How are you feeling, boss?"

"Much better." Tina smiled. "I decided to go to L.A."

"Really? Are you going to be okay to fly?"

"Yes. My morning sickness is finally going away."

"But what about?" Lisa patted her tummy.

"Gerta said it's fine to fly. Besides, I'm going to be flying all over in the sleigh on Christmas Eve," Tina said. "If I can do that, I can certainly take a plane to L.A."

"You're going to be really pregnant by Christmas Eve. Are you sure you can do the delivery?"

"Sure. Why not?"

"Is it safe for the baby?" Lisa persisted.

"I wouldn't do it if it weren't."

"Yeah, but it just seems… it always takes so much out of you."

"I'll be fine. The only thing I'm worried about is the big storm we're supposed to have."

"What if it happens when you're gone and you can't get back from L.A.? Or what if you go into labor early and can't do the delivery?" Lisa asked. "I don't think I could do it, and the suit is way too big for Walter."

Tina laughed. "And I thought I worried too much."

"Well, it could happen," Lisa said indignantly.

"Gerta said she might know more about the storm as it gets closer. And I'm doing the delivery just like I do every year as long as she says it's okay."

"Alrighty. I won't worry until you tell me to," Lisa said. "Anyway, it's Friday. Let's go to the pub tonight. We haven't been there in forever."

"I can't drink," Tina reminded her.

"I know, but isn't it karaoke night?" Lisa raised her eyebrows.

"That means the reindeer will be there and it will be loud and crowded and crazy."

"Sounds fun to me." Lisa beamed.

"Me too." Tina smiled.

***

Lisa ordered two more Polar Coladas. "We're lucky we got a booth tonight. It's a good thing we got here early."

Walter tipped his glass up to finish the last few drops of his drink. "Is it me or is Rudy a better singer tonight?"

"It's the Polar Colada." Tina giggled.

"Really? He sounds better to me too," Lisa marveled.

Just then, a blast of cold air hit them. A moving mountain of snow and ice slid past them, leaving a watery trail.

"Santina. Walter. Lisa," he said in his low rumbling voice.

"Hi, Abominable," Tina responded.

"Congratulations," he said.

"Thank you," Tina answered.

"Oh, Abe," Walter said. "Have you sensed any big storms coming?"

Abominable slowly turned to them, exhaling an icy gust. His coal-black eyes focused on them. "Nothing yet, but it's coming."

He continued slowly toward the cold room attached to the side of the building.

"Nice to see you," Lisa called.

The three of them shivered. An employee at the inn appeared with a mop.

"I don't know why they don't use the outside entrance," Conrad groused.

"I'll never get used to this place." Lisa giggled.

"Attention." Rudolph tapped on the microphone with his nose. "Can everyone hear me? Good. Remember, anyone who wants to sing needs to sign up.

In the meantime, I can start..."

"Oi, Rudy! Get off the stage!" Donner yelled. "Give someone else a go."

"Okay, maybe we can do a singalong," Rudolph said brightly.

"How about 'Dashing Through the Snow'?" Lisa shouted.

Dasher jumped up from his seat. "That's about me!"

"How many times do I have to tell you? That's not about you," Donner said.

"Who asked you?" Dasher demanded.

"Uh oh," Walter said. "I hope they don't get too rowdy."

"No throwing chairs tonight, Blitzen," Conrad warned from behind the bar.

"You heard him. Pipe down," Blitzen ordered.

"Singalong. Singalong," Rudolph chanted into the mic.

"I wish I could have a Peppermintini." Tina stirred her fruit juice with a straw.

"That drink always got you into trouble," Lisa said.

"I know." Tina smiled wistfully.

"How's your stomach?" Walter asked.

"I feel fine, but I think I'm getting a little bump." Tina pulled her sweater tight over her stomach. "See?"

"Oh, my gosh." Lisa clapped her hands. "A little mini-Tina or mini-George is in there. How cute."

"Are you going to find out what it is?" Walter asked.

Tina shook her head. "I don't want to know in advance. I want it to be a surprise."

"It's already a surprise." Lisa sipped her drink.

***

"Please talk to Isabella," George implored.

"I don't know what to say. She has issues," Nick responded.

"But your chemistry on stage was off again."

"That's not my fault." Nick signaled to the bartender

for another beer.

"You told her you're not interested in Skyler, right?"

"Right."

"She must not have believed you." George tapped his fingers on the bar absentmindedly. "Is Skyler coming to the concert in L.A.?"

Nick shrugged.

"It's going to piss off Isabella if she does."

"She's too high-maintenance."

"Which one?" George asked.

The server approached them. "Your table is ready."

They picked up their beers and followed him to a booth. They slid in opposite each other and accepted the menus he held out to them.

"I'm glad we decided to go out for dinner. It's nice to get away from the guys for a while," George said. "Tina is coming to the show in L.A. So is Gemma."

"And Courtney," Nick added.

"John will be happy to see her."

George glanced up from his menu and did a double take. Isabella and Lilliana were seated a few booths down behind Nick. Isabella's back was to them, but he caught Lilliana's eye and she quickly looked away. He wondered whether they should ask them to join them. Probably not a good idea. Should they send over drinks? Lilliana glanced his way again and slightly shook her head. Probably best not to stir things up.

They ordered and handed the menus back to the server.

"Isabella's got too many issues," Nick commented. "She's a total drama queen."

"It's probably because she likes you."

Nick smiled and caught himself.

"Hey, you know what would be great?" George said. "Total subject change."

"What?" Nick leaned back in the booth and drank his beer.

"I think you should come to the festival this year," George said. "Seriously. We could fly up together."

"No way, man. I'm not flying up there twice."

"What do you mean, twice?"

"I'm probably going to Kai's wedding. We grew up together."

"Oh, yeah. I forgot about that. Guess I'm going too."

They suddenly heard high-pitched squeals. "I told you it was them," a female voice said.

"It's Nick! And George!"

A server intercepted them.

"It's okay," George said and waved the young girls over. "Do you want autographs or selfies? I don't have a pen or paper. Do you?" He looked at Nick.

Nick shook his head.

"I do," one of the girls said and handed George a pen and scraps of paper from her purse.

"You guys are so dope!" the other girl gushed.

"Thanks." George gave them a smile and signed two pieces of paper and handed them to Nick, who did the same.

Then the girls took selfies with the guys. George noticed Isabella and Lilliana watching them.

"Do you like *Rock Goddess*?" he asked the girls.

"We love *Rock Goddess*!" one of them cried emphatically.

"You can get their autographs too." He pointed.

The girls squealed again and hurried off, giggling. Nick twisted around and ran his fingers through his spiky white hair.

"Now she's following me," he groaned. "She's so hung up on me and is totally in denial about it."

25 *Chick Chat*

Tina's stomach jumped with anticipation as she exited the plane.

"We're going to see your daddy," she whispered, patting her tummy.

Her eyes darted amongst the crowd milling at the LAX baggage claim. She saw George waving his arms at her and they pushed their way toward each other. He wore sunglasses and a black baseball hat with his dark hair pulled back into a ponytail. He pulled Tina into his arms and they squeezed each other tightly. He gave her a quick kiss.

"Let's get your suitcase and get out of here." He grabbed her hand and led the way.

"When is Gemma getting in?" she asked.

"Gemma will be here tonight, and Courtney got here this morning." He glanced back at her with a smile. "I guess us guys will have to be on our best behavior."

They found a spot by the luggage carousel. Tina shook off the heavy coat she'd worn boarding the plane at North Pole International Airport and held it draped over her arm.

George looked down and placed his hand on her stomach. "You're getting a little bigger."

Tina nodded happily. "You're going to be a daddy."

"You're going to be a mommy. I still can't believe it. How was the flight? Are you okay?"

"Yes. I feel fine."

The luggage carousel started up and drew their attention. People pushed in closer, jostling them. After watching it go round and round a few times, George recognized Tina's flowered suitcase and grabbed it. He lifted the handle, and they headed toward the exit.

"Your suitcase is light," he noticed.

"I know. I don't have my summer clothes up north. They're at the condo. I might have to buy some."

"We have plenty of *Black Ice* T-shirts." He grinned.

Tina sighed as soon as they exited the building. She squinted at the brightness and admired the palm trees and blue skies. It was hot out but felt good after the chill of the North Pole.

"Where are your sunglasses?" George asked.

Tina was glad she had remembered them. George took her coat and draped it over her suitcase while she rummaged in her purse until she found the eyeglass case. She put the large framed sunglasses on and felt all her tension seep away as she followed George to the rental car. She was so happy she'd decided to come. It was good to see her husband. It had been way too long.

***

"I have stuff you can borrow," Courtney offered while they got ready for dinner in the bathroom in Tina and George's hotel room. "I know I'm taller, but you can borrow some tops. I don't know if my shorts will fit you."

"I have a cute sundress you can wear. It's loose," Gemma said. "It'll be comfortable. I'll go get it."

"That sounds good," Tina said.

"Ooh. We can go shopping tomorrow and get you some maternity clothes," Courtney said.

"Here's the dress." Gemma returned and held it up. It was a flowing floral dress with thin straps that hung down to just below her knees. "I was actually going to give it to you. It's not my style."

Courtney appraised it. "You could wear it with a belt until you get bigger."

"It's great. Thanks." Tina beamed at Gemma. "Aunt Gemma."

"Okay, girlfriend." Courtney frowned at Gemma. "What's the deal with you and Loren? Spill."

Gemma smiled coyly. "We're just having fun. That's all. It's not a big thing."

Courtney watched Tina pull the dress over her head and turned back to Gemma. "Come on."

"Really," Gemma insisted. "I don't want a serious

thing." The corners of her mouth pulled up. "I do really like him, though. He's cute, isn't he?"

"Oh, yeah, he is." Courtney nodded.

"What do you think of the dress? I like it." Tina twirled. "It's comfortable."

"Cute," Courtney said.

"It's more your style. It looks good on you." Gemma nodded.

"Loren really likes you," Tina said.

"I know." Gemma grinned. "Is it true he was involved with your friend Lisa?"

"That was when she had a misunderstanding with Walter. They just went out a few times. It was no big deal."

"He had a thing with Isabella too," Courtney said.

"No, he didn't," Tina said. "He was just messing with Nick because he likes her."

"That's not what I heard." Courtney leaned toward the mirror to put on mascara.

Gemma and Tina looked at each other. "What did you hear?" Gemma asked. Then she shook her head and held her hand out. "No. Don't tell me. It doesn't matter."

Good for Gemma, Tina thought, despite her own curiosity. But no, rumors usually weren't true. She remembered when Nick and Isabella had generated publicity by pretending to be a couple. That had all been fabricated, though she knew Nick had hoped for it to become a reality.

Gemma fluffed her hair in the mirror as Courtney applied glittery eyeshadow to Tina's eyelids.

"We are going to rock L.A. tonight!" Courtney proclaimed. "With our rock star guys!"

***

"What do you want, Nick?" Isabella opened her hotel room door all the way to grant him entry.

Lilliana was on the phone.

"Peace, okay?" Nick said hopefully. He still didn't get why she seemed so mad at him.

"Where's your new little friend?"

He peered at her blankly.

"Skyler." She shook her head.

He shrugged.

"Is she coming to the show tonight?"

Lilliana hung up the phone. "Meet you downstairs in half an hour, Is." She closed the door behind her on her way out.

"I don't know," Nick answered.

That reminded him. He should text her.

Isabella stood in front of the wide window. The lights of the city sparkled below.

Nick went over to the window and scanned the skyline. "Savage view."

"Just say what you want to say already," Isabella said.

"Uh, our chemistry is off." He turned to her. "The fans love it when we sing together, but you're all mad at me. I don't get it. Peace, okay?"

She moaned in frustration. "You're right. I can't let this affect my performance. The fans deserve better."

"Right."

Isabella stood with her hands on her hips, staring at him. "You have no idea, do you? You're totally clueless."

"About what?"

"You and me. We've had this little dance going on and you don't even know it."

"What dance?" What was she going on about? Another musical?

"All this time we've spent together and you don't really know me, do you?"

"I know you." How could he be standing here talking to her if he didn't know her?

"You have all this passion and intensity, but you don't know how to relate it to someone," Isabella said.

"I can totally relate it," he retorted. Whatever that

meant.

"Okay, then. How do we fix this?"

"Just quit being mad at me."

Isabella shook her head again and turned toward the window, gazing out.

Wow, she was high-maintenance. He racked his brain. What did she want him to say? What could he say that would make her act nice to him again? He really could think of no rational reason for her acting so mean and stubborn. She'd gotten over him grabbing and kissing her that time, even though he'd read her signals right, but then she got all bent out of shape when Skyler showed up. That wasn't his fault. He couldn't help who his fans were. Maybe she was jealous because his band was becoming more successful, or maybe she was upset that this was their last tour together and she was afraid they wouldn't see each other anymore.

"I'll still come to your house after the tour," he assured her. "I'll still write songs with you like 'Last Song.'"

"It's a beautiful song." Her eyes met his. "You're really an enigma."

"Thanks." It sounded like a compliment.

She turned back to the window.

"Hey, I know your mother freaks you out. My family is a freakout too." Maybe that was it.

"You have a great family. I like your sister, and George is your brother-in-law now."

"Right. But growing up, my parents expected me to take over the family business, and they put all this pressure on me and I couldn't be myself. I couldn't do what I wanted until I got away."

Isabella turned toward him. "I told you my mother wanted me to teach music. She thought my songs were silly and I couldn't sing."

"She's whacked."

Isabella smiled. "Thanks, Nicky."

She hadn't called him that in a while.

***

"Nick! That was great! Your song with Isabella was awesome!" Tina couldn't help gushing like a fan backstage. "The audience is going crazy. The show has gotten better since I saw it last time." She grabbed him into a hug even though he was sweaty.

He hugged her back and reached for water. "I get so dehydrated. It's hot onstage with all the lights."

"You didn't stop moving the entire time," she marveled.

"Right."

Tina glanced at the band members on the other side of the room with Courtney and Gemma and lowered her voice.

"Are things okay with you and Isabella now? It looked like it when you sang together."

"I don't get that woman," he griped. "You're a woman. What's up?"

"Tell her how you feel about her," Tina advised. "Just tell her already."

"She's hung up on me and she won't admit it."

"Nick!" Tina took a deep breath. "This is your last tour together. Just tell her and either she feels the same way or she doesn't. Then, at least, you'll know and you can move on either way."

"She's playing games with me. Two can play and I'm going to win this."

"It's not a game, Nick," Tina emphasized. "Tell her before the tour is over. Otherwise, you might never see her again."

"She'll come to me." He nodded confidently.

George came over and put his arm around Tina.

"Please tell Nick to just talk to Isabella before he blows it," Tina said to him.

"You heard her," George told Nick. "I agree with her."

"You have to agree with her," Nick said.

"Let's go out for drinks," Courtney called to them.

"Can't drink." Tina patted her tummy.

"We're going back to the hotel so I can be alone with my wife." George took Tina's hand and pulled her away.

"Come on, Nick." Loren waved his arm.

"Right." He followed them, but then Isabella appeared in the doorway.

"Can I talk to you?" she asked.

"Just catch up with us," John said. "I'll text you when we decide where we're going."

"Let's just hit the hotel bar," Milo suggested. He pulled the door shut behind them.

"Great show tonight," Isabella said breathlessly. "Our song was... you're just electric on stage."

"You're magical," he responded.

Isabella had a spell over him, and he couldn't shake it. She was fogging his mind.

"Our chemistry comes out when we're onstage," she said with a smile. "My adrenaline is still going... and it's connected to you."

His eyes met hers. He couldn't move or speak. She was drawing him in again and he was helpless.

"Nick," she whispered. "Is this real?"

He was lost in the deepness of her eyes. He put his water bottle down.

"I realized on stage tonight that you do understand me on a subconscious level," Isabella murmured. "The way we move together in sync and the way our voices complement each other. Opposites are magnetic. We're drawn together. We can't help it."

Nick wasn't sure he was getting what she was saying, but she was drawing closer. He could smell her sweat mixed with that musky vanilla scent she wore. It was overwhelming and intoxicating. But this time, he would control himself. It was her move.

"Nicky." Her voice was soft, barely audible.

Isabella put her hands on either side of his face and pulled him to her. Their lips met. This was exactly what he'd been waiting for. He knew she'd come to him. She couldn't help herself, and she'd just admitted it. And this time it wasn't for publicity. This time, it was real.

26 *Intriguing & Intoxicating*

"That shower really relaxed me." George pulled back the blankets and got into bed. "But I'm still wide awake."

"Me too," Tina said. She cuddled up to him in her *Black Ice* T-shirt. "I miss sleeping with you."

"I miss it too." He rested his hand on her tummy. "I keep thinking about what it will be like."

"We have to think of names. Does it have to be a G name? Your parents like G names."

"No. Garrett and Tonia named their son Evan. We can pick whatever name we like. Should we name it after one of our parents?"

"Let's see. Gloria. Grover. Nicholas. Clara," Tina said. "Maybe we can use one of those for a middle name."

"Yeah. What about the last name? You kept your name when we got married, but what about the baby?"

"Hmm," Tina thought. "We could give it your last name except..."

"It has to have the name Claus if it becomes the next Santa," George finished her sentence.

Tina sat up. "Does that bother you?"

George placed a pillow behind him and leaned against it.

"Is it going to take over only if it's a girl? How does it work?"

"The original Santa was supposed to be a woman, and I broke tradition by being the first female Santa, but I guess it could be Santa either way. I was just talking to Gerta about this."

"What if he or she doesn't want the job like Nick?" he asked.

Tina frowned. "I see the dilemma my parents had, but I wouldn't want to force this on a kid. It's a huge commitment. Our child will have to choose to become Santa."

"Guess we'll have to have more than one just to be on the safe side." George grinned.

"Oh," Tina remembered. "Gerta said we'll have more than one child, but we've never really talked about it. How many do you want?"

"Well, we both have busy careers and I've never wanted more than two, because there are enough people on the planet."

"Tell me about it. There are more kids to deliver to every year."

"You would know then. Does two sound good to you?"

"Two sounds perfect."

"We have to think of a boy's name and a girl's name because we don't know what we're having," George said. "Are there some sort of Claus guidelines or something? Your brother was named after your father, and so were you."

"Yeah. Nicholas Junior and Santina. But we're not going there. We can choose whatever name we want. No G names and no Santa names."

"Agreed."

"I'm going to hyphenate my last name and we can do the same with the baby," Tina said decisively.

"Are you sure?" George asked. "Claus-Garner?"

"Yes. I want your name, George. I should have done it sooner."

"That makes me happy, Mrs. Garner."

"I like the sound of that," she said.

"This is going to get more difficult once we have kids, you know. Going back and forth between the North Pole and Florida with kids."

Tina bit her lip. "Especially once they start school. I don't know what we'll do then."

"That's a long way off. We'll figure it out. Come here." George pulled her to him. "I missed you and we're finally alone."

***

Nick answered his phone. "I've been trying to reach you. When do you want me to come to L.A.? We're in Seattle now. This is our last city on the tour."

"That's why I'm calling," Skyler said. "My agent has another project for me. He didn't really like the scientist idea."

"Why not?" Nick asked. "It's brilliant."

"He said nobody would buy me as a scientist."

"That's crap."

"I know. Right? Why couldn't I be a scientist?" She let out a sigh. "He likes the Santina idea well enough, but he said I'm not ready to play a lead. He wants me to take some smaller roles first, even though I've already done three films."

"Bummer."

"That's Hollywood." Skyler sighed again. "I'll let you know if I want to work on the screenplay about the scientist. I still like the idea, but I don't know. First, I have to go back to England to do this other movie."

"I could still do the music for your movies," Nick offered.

"This director usually uses the same person to score all his films, but I'll keep you in mind," she said, sounding distracted. "I really must go, Nick. I have to read this boring script."

"Right." Nick disconnected the call.

This was disappointing, but that's Hollywood, as Skyler had said.

"Who was that?" Isabella asked from the couch in her dressing room, staring down at her phone.

"Skyler."

"Oh." She wrinkled her nose.

"Her agent wants her to do another movie instead of the scientist one," he told her.

"Does that mean you're not going to L.A.?"

"Right."

"I know that's a disappointment, Nicky." Isabella rose and came over to him. "It would've been a fantastic opportunity to score a movie, but maybe this is a good thing. In the meantime, you can learn more about it if that's what you want to do."

"I should focus on the band."

"I think that's best right now. *Black Ice* is going to be the headliner on your next tour. You need to get ready for that. Things are happening for the band."

"Right."

"And we'll have a break between tours. I really need to rest and work on new material."

Isabella ran her fingers along his arm and turned his chin to look at her. Nick fell into her eyes as always. He was more helpless than ever under her spell.

"What is it about you?" she asked. "You're not like anybody else. Your white hair. Your righteous anger. Your intensity. Your passion. There's nobody like you, Nicky. You intrigue me."

"You intoxicate me," Nick replied.

Isabella smiled. "This is going to be interesting."

***

"Why do I have so many emails?" Tina groaned.

"Oh, I asked people to RSVP for the festival, but I was using your computer, so you're getting all the responses," Lisa said. "Sorry."

"Should I just forward them to you?"

"No, I'll get on your computer every day and delete them. I have to match them to my spreadsheet for the guests." Lisa took a deep breath. "I can't tell you how busy I've been while you were gone."

"With the plans for the festival?" Tina asked.

"I always have to outdo myself from the year before," Lisa said. "I set a high bar, you know."

"You always do an outstanding job."

"Thanks. And this year I have an entire team of volunteers helping, but we can't seem to come up with any new ideas."

"There's still lots of time," Tina said. "It'll be great."

"Yeah." Lisa shrugged. "How was your trip? You look a lot more relaxed. In fact..." She stepped closer. "I believe you're glowing."

"It's because I got some sun." Tina blushed. "It was so nice to see George, and the concert was incredible. Nick was just amazing. I'm so glad I went."

"Did Skyler show up?"

"No. But Courtney was there, and so was Gemma. She gave me this cute dress because I didn't have anything to wear. All my summer clothing is in Florida," Tina said. "And we went shopping for maternity clothes and I got a bunch of cute stuff."

"I can't imagine you with a fat tummy."

"I know." Tina suddenly gasped. "I forgot to tell you."

"What? What?" Lisa sat on the chair opposite Tina's desk and dragged it close.

"Nick and Isabella." Tina pressed her lips together.

"What about them?"

"Nick and Isabella," Tina repeated slowly.

"No way! Really?" Lisa's mouth fell open.

"For real this time." Tina nodded.

"They're probably just pretending for publicity again for the tour."

"It's not for publicity. I never thought it would really happen." Tina shook her head. "I'm happy for Nick."

Lisa crossed her arms. "I give it till the end of the tour."

***

"Start growing your beard," Clara said, reading her email.

"You keep saying that. It doesn't take that long to grow," Santa grumbled.

She glanced at him. "I guess not."

"What's the plan?" he asked.

She looked back at the email from Tina. "George is flying up next week. We'll go up the week after."

"Are you sure? We're going to be up there for a long time."

"I just can't wait. I have to see Tina. She needs me."

"She doesn't need you. She has George."

"A woman needs her mother when she's expecting," Clara said adamantly. "Now don't argue with me."

"Tina's doing a fine job with the business."

"Yes, she is, but we've been putting too much pressure on her."

"What pressure? We haven't put any pressure on her."

"I think I have," Clara confessed. "I was worried I made you retire too early, and I thought you wanted your old job back."

"Who said anything about that?" he asked. "Sure, I miss it sometimes, but going up for a few months a year takes care of that."

"Don't you get bored being retired?"

"I get bored sometimes, but Tina has everything under control. I guess she was right about updating a few things." He jabbed a finger at her. "But don't tell her I said that."

Clara beamed. "I'm so proud of her. I wonder if we can get Nick to come up for the festival or for Thanksgiving and have the whole family together."

Santa waved his hand at her. "Good luck with that."

"I have so much to do before we go. I should go to the mall with Myra and buy some baby things. Tina will need so much. I bet she doesn't have anything yet," Clara said. "Except the girls took her shopping for maternity clothes."

Santa settled into his chair and pointed the remote at the TV.

"I might have to buy another suitcase for everything." Clara mused out loud.

"Hmm." Santa flipped through the channels.

***

"Thanks, Fritz."

George paid the snow taxi driver and lugged his two suitcases upstairs to the apartment. The wind was biting cold, and he squinted against the frosty bits of ice pelting him. Tina opened the door and helped him in.

"I could've met you at the airport." She gave him a quick kiss.

"There's no need for you to go out in this weather," he assured her. He hung up his coat and pulled off his boots. "I forget how cold it is here."

He hurried over to stand in front of the gas fireplace while Tina rolled his suitcases into the bedroom and returned to the living room. She put her arms around him and he put a hand on her tummy.

"You're bigger."

"I think I feel it moving."

"Yeah?"

"Sometimes I feel this little fluttering. I think it's the baby." She couldn't help squealing with delight.

"Wow, are you wearing maternity pants?"

"My pants are too tight now. I can still wear my sweatpants and sweatshirts. They're pretty comfortable," she said. "Are you hungry? I have a casserole in the oven."

"It smells good. I'm starving. Airport food sucks. It's hard to find vegetarian food."

"The casserole's done. I'm just keeping it warm. Let's eat."

Tina placed plates and silverware on the table and set the casserole in the middle.

"Nick said he's coming up for the wedding." George pulled out a chair and sat down.

"He is? I hope he stays for Thanksgiving. That would make my parents happy." Tina sat opposite him. "What about Gemma? Does she still want to come up?"

"She does, but she still doesn't believe where we are or who you are. I'm just going to buy her ticket and let her find out when she gets here."

"She's in for a surprise." Tina smiled.

"It's going to blow her mind." George grinned at her.

"We're going to have a full house. I wonder where we'll put everyone." Tina tapped her chin. "We have Nick's room, but if Gemma and Nick come at the same time…"

"He's not coming until November, so maybe she can come right after the festival."

"That works. It won't be too crazy yet. I hope Nick helps while he's here. We can always use the help."

"He probably won't want to stay too long, now that he and Isabella are together."

"Oh, my gosh! I forgot about that," Tina said. "How are they doing?"

"So far, so good."

"I'm glad. What about Gemma and Loren?"

"As far as I know, everything is good with them, too."

"He seems more serious than she is."

"Who knows?" George shrugged.

Tina shook her head. "What a soap opera."

27 *Claustrophobia*

"I'm sorry," Lisa said, pulling her suitcase into the apartment. "We shouldn't be here too long."

"This is really nice of you." Walter carried a small suitcase behind her. "I hate to put you out."

"Not at all," Tina said. "We're happy to have you."

"You two haven't seen each other for months, and now we're barging in. I told Lisa we were intruding and should go to the Snowed Inn & Pub." Walter set down his suitcase.

"Don't be silly. The inn would be a terrible commute every day," Tina said.

"The work shouldn't take longer than a week," Walter said.

"Don't worry about it, Walter," George assured him. "You're welcome as long as it takes."

"What kind of work are they doing in the house?" Tina asked.

"They're raising all the doorways," Lisa answered. "And they're going to raise the ceiling into the crawlspace in the living room and kitchen."

"That sounds complicated," Tina said.

"They've renovated houses like this before," Walter said. "We're not the first mixed-height couple."

"It's going to be so nice to have some room. I always feel so squished in that house," Lisa said. "We talked about buying another house, but this was much less expensive and I didn't want to make Walter sell his house."

"It's probably going to raise the heating bill a little with a higher ceiling," Walter said. "But I want Lisa to feel comfortable."

"I like the house. It's small and cozy, but the low ceilings just make it feel too claustrophobic," Lisa explained.

Walter sighed. "It's going to be expensive, but we have to make sacrifices for the ones we love."

"Compromises," George said. "But it's worth it."

"When are your parents getting here?" Lisa asked.

"Next Thursday," Tina answered.

Walter furrowed his brow. "We'll just go to the inn if the work isn't finished. They told me it won't take more than a week at the most."

"Worst case, we can all stay here," Tina insisted. "There are three bedrooms."

"We could do it for a few days if we need to," Lisa said to Walter.

He frowned.

"Don't worry, Walter. It'll be worth it," she said.

He took a deep breath. "You're right."

"It's really great to see you two. Let's go out to dinner at the Kringle Café," George suggested.

"Great idea," Tina said enthusiastically. "I'm going to get ready." George followed her into their bedroom.

"Our treat," Walter called.

"Thanks, Walter." Lisa hugged him. "I know change is hard for you, but I really appreciate your hiring those contractors. It means a lot to me."

"I just can't wait until they finish so we can be back in our own house again," he muttered.

"We've only been here five minutes, Walter," Lisa said. "Think of it this way. We're going to have a big slumber party every night." She giggled. "Isn't this fun?"

***

Nick couldn't believe how lucky he was. Every time Isabella smiled at him, his mind fogged up like the mirror in a bathroom after a hot shower. She had this effect on him. He couldn't stop thinking about her when they were apart, and her voice on the phone made him weak. It was crazy. And scary. She had this power over him. It was thrilling. It was almost better than being on stage with fans screaming for him. Sometimes it was better. In fact, it *was* better. What was happening to him?

"Hello?" Kris waved a hand in front of his face.

"Huh?" Nick was on his couch.

"Uh oh. This guy's in love." Milo shook his head.

"Give him a break," John said.

"It's awesome, Nick," Loren said.

"You never want to hang out anymore," Kris whined.

"Get more beer," Nick ordered.

Kris obediently went into the kitchen. "There's only five bottles left," he yelled.

"Bring them," Milo instructed.

"How many new songs do we have for the album and the tour?" Loren took control of the band meeting.

"We have three," Milo said, looking at John for confirmation.

Kris picked up their empty beer bottles and brought them into the kitchen.

"How many does George have?" Loren asked.

"He has three," Nick said.

"How many do you have?" Loren asked him.

"Seven."

"I hope they're not all about Isabella." Milo rolled his eyes.

Nick contemplated.

"You're losing your edge," Milo complained. "Our image is not a bunch of guys in love."

"Milo's right," Loren said. "I hope you have some songs for our hardcore fans."

"Right."

"I could write some songs," Kris offered, returning from the kitchen.

"You write songs?" Milo scowled at him.

"I could do it," Kris said defensively. "What's so hard about it?"

"Show us what you've got then," John said.

"I will," Kris said.

Milo waved his hand at him dismissively.

"I still got my edge because I'm not a wimp like you guys," Kris said. "I'm still single, like Milo. I won't let some lame girl tell me what to do.”

“Good for you.” John humored him.

“So, is this the real thing with Isabella?” Milo asked Nick.

“Yeah,” Nick responded.

“Just when we’re about to go on separate tours?” Milo chuckled. “Bad timing, man.”

“We’re not touring until next year,” John said.

“But *Rock Goddess* is going to Europe in a few months, aren’t they?” Loren asked.

“I have to go to a wedding up north in November,” Nick remembered.

“Weird time for a wedding,” John noted.

“What’s that bell sound?” Kris asked.

“My phone.” Nick pulled his phone from his pocket. He peered at the caller ID and grinned.

“It must be Isabella,” Milo said. “Summoning him.”

***

“Your turn.” Tina came out of the bathroom wearing her pink bathrobe and matching fuzzy slippers.

“It sucks having one bathroom.” Lisa stood in the hallway between the bedrooms.

“Can you imagine when Nick and I were little and we all lived here?” Tina shook her head. “I didn’t really think about it at the time.”

“At least the guys are letting us use the bathroom first to get ready for work.”

“Where are they?” Tina asked.

“They’re watching the morning news on TV,” Lisa said. “And George is making breakfast, so I’m not going to complain. It’s kind of like being in a hotel with room service.”

“At least we all get along,” Tina said. She headed to the living room.

“Morning, Tina.” Walter was seated at the table eating pancakes, facing the TV.

“What’s on the news this morning?” Tina asked.

"The weather just keeps getting crazier." Walter shook his head.

George came out of the kitchen and set a plate on the table. He gave Tina a kiss. "Taking turns showering and eating seems to work."

"Thanks." Tina smiled at George. "I'm hungry."

"Eating for two," Walter commented.

"I'll clean up when everyone is finished eating," she told George.

"I can do it. All of you have to go to work," he said.

Tina looked over at the TV. "Floods in some states and fires in others. Those poor people."

"All of us in the band donated money to the Red Cross," George said.

"That's wonderful. What a great idea," Tina said.

"I'm going to go into the office." Walter set his fork on his plate.

"Don't you want to take a shower?" Tina asked.

"We ran out of hot water when we all took showers yesterday morning," he said. "You and Lisa can take showers in the morning, and I'll take one at night."

"I'll take one during the day while you're all at work," George said.

"I'm sorry, Walter," Tina said. "I didn't know..."

"It's no big deal. Taking a shower at night relaxes me and helps me sleep," he said. He put on his shoes and left.

"I feel so bad," Tina said. "It didn't occur to me we'd run out of hot water."

"I hate not having any privacy," George said, sitting down to eat.

"By the time they leave, my parents will be here," Tina said. "We won't have any time alone."

"Maybe we should've let them go to the inn."

"No. It would've been too far for them to come to work every day. I'm glad we could help them out, but it's hard with all of us here."

"I'm not used to cooking for four people every day. I'll have to go shopping again, but I have to go anyway because your parents will be here," George said. "At least your mother cooks, too."

"I wish Lisa would pick up her towels. She doesn't clean up after herself," Tina said. "I wonder if Walter has to pick up after her."

"Why don't you just ask him?" Lisa said from the doorway.

Tina's eyes widened.

"I know we're in the way," Lisa said tersely. "We'll leave today."

"But what about your house?" Tina asked.

"I'm sure we can stay there while they work on it. We'll just have to breathe in all the dust." She went into the kitchen.

Tina put her hand over her mouth and looked at George.

"Lisa, you know you and Walter are always welcome here," George called.

"Sorry, we're eating all your food up."

Lisa came out of the kitchen with a plate of pancakes. She spread butter and poured syrup over them.

"If you don't mind, I'll take this to Walter's office and eat it." She picked up a fork.

"You're wearing your slippers," Tina noticed.

"Who cares? I'm just going down the hall," Lisa said. "Unless we have a dress code I'm not aware of."

"Lisa..."

"I'll see you at the office." She strode to the door and exited.

***

Tina went into her office to turn on her computer. She'd been going over and over in her head what to say to Lisa and Walter. As soon as she entered her password, she was going to go into his office and apologize to both of them.

"Do you want tea?" Lisa appeared in her doorway.

"Okay, but I want to talk to you."

"I'll get your tea, boss." Lisa turned to leave. "There's nothing to talk about unless it's about work."

"No. I just..."

"I'll get your tea." She was quickly gone.

Tina let out a big sigh. She went next door to Walter's office.

"I'm sorry we're in your way," he said from behind his desk. "We'll be out today. I'm waiting for the contractor to call me back to see if we can stay there while they work or we'll go to the inn."

"Walter, I don't know what Lisa told you, but of course you're welcome to stay with us for as long as you want. I just..."

Walter held up his hand. "No need to explain."

"Good." She was glad Walter was more reasonable.

"I'll just get back to work if there's nothing else," he said formally.

"Oh, my gosh!" Tina exclaimed. "You know I love you guys. It's just..."

"Tina, can I speak to you?" Rusty said from the doorway. "I'm sorry. Am I interrupting?"

"No," Walter said.

Tina walked back to her office, and Rusty sauntered after her. She sat behind her desk.

"What can I do for you, Rusty?"

"Are you feeling okay?" he asked. "You look tired."

"I'm fine. Thank you."

"I just need a signature on this requisition form. Jamie looked at the mail chute and she thinks we need to replace one of the panels. It got bent somehow," he explained.

"Bent? How could it get bent?"

He shrugged. "It's pretty old. Maybe they get warped over time."

"You don't need my signature to fix it."

"I know, but I wanted to let you know because the panel is pretty expensive," he said. "We have to special order it and it wasn't in the budget."

"Okay." Tina signed the form.

"You know, we're getting a lot of letters," Rusty said. "You should come down and read some before you get too busy."

"That's a good idea. I always enjoy reading the letters."

"Here's your tea." Lisa came in and set a mug on her desk. "I'll be working in Walter's office."

"Okay, but if you have time today, I'd like you to go down to the mailroom and read some letters," Tina said. "Rusty said they're getting a lot of mail and could use some help."

Lisa turned to Rusty. "Oh, hey. You need some help?"

"If you're not too busy," he said. "We can always use more readers."

"Okay. I guess I can read letters for a few hours today." Lisa sighed.

28 *Not Thursday*

Tina answered her office phone.

"Did you talk to them?" George asked.

"I tried to apologize, but they wouldn't listen," Tina said dejectedly. "I sent Lisa down to the mailroom. I'm going to talk to her there..."

"Your parents are here."

"What? What are they doing here? They're not supposed to be here until Thursday."

"Here's your mother." George handed the phone to Clara.

"Hi, Tina. How are you feeling?" Clara asked.

"Mom, what are you doing here? You told me Thursday."

"I thought I told you we got an earlier flight," Clara said.

"I thought you meant earlier in the day."

"Oh. Well..."

"Lisa and Walter are staying with us. They have contractors at their house."

"I know. George told us," Clara said. "We'll make do. It's only for a day or two, right?"

"I guess so," Tina said. "We didn't even get a chance to wash the sheets for you or go food shopping."

"Now don't worry. I'll wash the sheets, and George and I are making a grocery list."

"Mom, I wish you would've told me you were coming today. I had everything planned for Thursday."

"Now don't you worry about anything," Clara insisted. "We're here to help, so just go about your day and we'll see you later."

"Okay."

"Could you come home for lunch?" she asked. "I just can't wait to see you."

"I was planning to, anyway."

"Good. We'll see you in a few hours. I'm going to wash the sheets and clean the bathroom. Somebody left towels all over the floor," Clara said. "What time will you be home for lunch?"

"Around noon."

"I'll have everything done by then, and George and I will go food shopping after you leave. Though maybe we should do that first. It's always better to get there earlier in the day. They have a better selection. It's hard to get fresh produce here."

"I'll see you later, Mom."

Tina hung up the phone and let out a deep sigh. Why hadn't Lisa picked up her towels in the bathroom? And why hadn't George done it? Hadn't he gone into the bathroom after them?

She went next door to Walter's office and tapped lightly on the open door.

He looked up. "Tina."

"Walter, I don't want to fight with you guys. This is silly. Lisa overheard us venting about privacy or something. I don't even remember what we said, but you know we're happy to have you."

He nodded. "I appreciate it, but it stresses me out not being home. I'm still waiting to hear back from the contractor."

"Well, things just got more crowded at my place. My parents are here."

"I thought they were coming on Thursday."

"That's what my mother told me, but they changed their plans. I don't remember her telling me about it." Tina shook her head.

"Okay..."

Tina bit her lip. "You guys can stay as long as you need to. Don't worry about it. It will be a little tight, but it's fine. I mean it. Please stay."

"Thanks, Tina. It won't be much longer. A day or two."

"I know. I'm going down to the mailroom to talk to Lisa. I hate when she's mad at me."

"Good luck." Walter smiled sympathetically.

Tina always took the stairs. She certainly got her

exercise walking around this immense building. Hopefully, she wouldn't miss Lisa if she took the elevator back upstairs.

Tina heard a loud whoosh as she entered the mailroom. Mail had come down a chute into a large bin on wheels. She saw Lisa sitting at the end of a long row of workstations, each one occupied by an elf. Tina rolled over a chair and sat beside her.

Lisa looked up, glanced at the letter in her hand, and clicked her mouse while squinting at the computer. "We need more help."

"I'll send my parents down here. My father really enjoyed reading the letters last year," Tina said.

Lisa placed the letter on a pile and picked up the next one.

"Speaking of my parents," Tina said. "They're here."

"Have I been down here that long?"

Tina laughed. "No. They got here early."

"We'll get out of your hair then."

"I already talked to Walter," Tina said. "I just want to apologize if George and I made it sound like we don't want you staying with us. Of course, we all like our privacy, but you know I'd do anything for you and Walter."

Lisa read the letter in her hand.

Tina picked up the next one in the pile and pulled the letter out of the envelope.

Dear Santa,
I been the goodest I ever been in my life this year. Please please please get me Spiderman pajamas. And my mom wants a new refrigerator.
Adam

Tina handed it to Lisa, who studied the spreadsheet. Tina picked up the next one.

Hi Santa,
You are my favorite superhero. We don't have a chimney

so can you get into my house? I want a remote control car like my neighbor. But I want a blue one, not a red one. Then we can tell them apart.
Jose

"I'm a superhero." Tina showed the letter to Lisa.
Lisa pulled one from her pile. "Read this one."

I love you Santa. I don't think you're too fat. I like cookies too. I want a little sister or brother to play with. But make it a sister. And make sure nobody likes her better than me. I promise to be nice to her and share my toys. I will not lie or hit anyone.
Love, Tameka

Tina giggled. Lisa giggled with her. Tina opened another one.

Dear Santa,
I'm not sure you're real. Can I visit you to see? My friend said you are make believe like the tooth fairy. But if you're real, I want a new best friend. Could you get me a kitten too? I want the biggest tree ever too. Then I will believe in you.
Shannon

Tina held a letter in front of her and said out loud, "Dear Santa, please make my best friend not mad at me anymore. I promise not to bug her about picking up her towels. I'm so lucky to have such a great friend and I'd be lost without her."

Lisa playfully shoved her. "Okay. Okay. You got me in a good mood and now I can't be mad at you."

Tina groaned. "Do you believe my parents showed up early? I don't know if I'm ready for them yet. I have to go home for lunch because my mother wants to see me."

"She wants to see your tummy," Lisa said.

***

"Tina, look at you!" Clara shrieked. "Look at your stomach. You're pregnant."

"That's right." Tina stood staring down at the bulge under her maternity top.

"Look at her, dear," Clara said to Santa. "She's showing. That's our little grandchild in there." She put her hand on Tina's stomach. "Oh! Was that a kick?"

"I think that's the strongest one I've felt," Tina said.

"You know your grandma, don't you?" Clara patted Tina's stomach.

George came over and put his hand on her stomach. "The baby's active." He smiled at Tina.

"Come sit down, Tina, and eat something. Are you tired? Have you been sleeping okay?" Clara asked.

"Hi, Dad." Tina gave Santa a hug and sat down at the table. "Yes, and no."

"I thought so. I brought some melatonin. It might help you sleep better."

"That's a good idea," George agreed.

"How's the business?" Santa sat at the table.

George set a glass of water in front of Tina, and she took a sip. "Good. We're having problems with one of the mail chutes, but we ordered a replacement panel."

"Any other issues?"

"Not so far."

He nodded. "How's the mail? Are they keeping up?"

Tina smiled at his subtle hint. "They always need help. You should go down tomorrow and read some letters, Dad."

"If they need me."

"Mom, you could help Lisa with the festival," Tina suggested. "They probably need help decorating."

"That would be fun," Clara said. She set a sandwich in front of Tina. "I'm going to make you a smoothie every morning before work. I can put all your vitamins and other healthy supplements in it."

"It's green," Santa said with a grimace.

"I know, but they taste good," Tina said. "I always like your smoothies, Mom. They help me recover after the delivery on Christmas Eve."

"Soon you're going to have a different type of delivery," Clara said with excitement. "Instead of delivering presents..."

"I have months to go, Mom."

Tina glanced down at her tummy and took a bite of her sandwich. She suddenly felt famished.

***

"I love our new house so much!" Lisa enthused. "I don't have to worry about hitting my head anymore."

She sat at the table in front of her computer in Tina's office.

"That's great."

Tina swiveled her chair around and saw some reindeer out by the main barn kicking around a red ball.

"Walter complains all the time that I don't pick up after myself. I shouldn't have been such a slob at your place."

Tina swiveled back around to look at her. "You're not a slob. You're just..."

"Okay. Let's hear this one." Lisa crossed her arms.

"Domestically challenged?"

"Ha! I'm going to tell Walter that one next time he complains about my cleaning skills. He's a real neat freak."

"I can't believe the festival is almost here," Tina said. "I'm starting to see some pretty colors in the sky."

"I love the Northern Lights," Lisa said. "But your mother is driving me a little crazy."

"You didn't tell me that."

"It's fine. You have enough on your mind and I can deal with her. She wants to do things her way, and I just have to humor her."

"Thanks."

"I like your mother. She's fun."

"I wonder how my father is doing in the mailroom," Tina said.

"He's driving Rusty crazy, of course." Lisa laughed. "But everybody loves your father, and they're happy to see him. He just tries to micro-manage everyone."

Tina absentmindedly rubbed her tummy.

"Not like you. You trust everybody to do their job and things are more relaxed," Lisa said. "Don't worry about your mother and father. They really are helping out. We need it this time of year when things get busier."

"Especially after the Northern Lights festival," Tina said. "That's when things really pick up."

"Never a dull moment." Lisa smiled.

"That's for sure."

"How's it at home with your parents there?"

Tina frowned. "It's a little crowded. George is wonderful with my parents, letting my mother take over the kitchen and my father take over the TV."

"Too bad they have to stay with you. You're right on top of each other," Lisa said.

"I'm just trying to focus on work."

"You should clear out that storage room upstairs and convert it into a mini apartment with a bedroom and kitchenette. There's already a bathroom off your mother's workout room," Lisa said. "You could add a shower."

"That's a great idea. I'll think about that for next year."

"I know a good contractor." Lisa smiled.

"Oh. The baby kicked. I love that feeling."

"How about Amber, Bethany, or Jasmine?"

"Who are they?"

"Baby names," Lisa said. "If it's a girl."

"Oh!" Tina's face lit up. "If it's a girl, George likes Charlotte or Tessa."

"Nice."

"I was thinking of Katina," Tina said. "Amaryllis was the wise woman who bestowed the Gift upon Gertrude so she could be the first Santa, but then she got poisoned. Katina was her daughter."

"I remember you telling me about that when you read the history." Lisa nodded.

"Or maybe we could use one of those names as a middle name if it's a girl."

"How about Beau or Seth, if it's a boy?"

"George likes Dustin or Tristan or Finn. I kind of like those too, but I'll add your names to our list," Tina said. "My parents keep suggesting names, too."

"Let's look at the top baby names on the internet." Lisa turned to her computer and typed in a search. She clicked a few times and studied the results. "Okay, different sites have different answers, but at the top of most lists we have Asher and Liam for boys and Olivia and Emma for girls."

"I like those names."

"Well, don't use them. They'll be too common," Lisa advised. "There were always other Lisas in my class and I hated it. Think of something unusual, but not too weird."

"Okay, Aunt Lisa."

29 *Intermission*

Nick wondered why Milo had called this emergency band meeting. The guys looked serious, and they kept glancing at each other as he entered Milo's house.

"Sit down, Nick," Milo said.

Nick sat on the blue-gray couch in the living room. "Are we having a band meeting?"

Milo perched on the edge of an ottoman. "Everyone from the band is here except George, so you could call it that."

"What's up?" Nick looked between them.

"It's an intermission!" Kris bellowed.

"Shut up, Kris," Milo said. "And it's intervention, which this is not."

"You know I don't do drugs," Nick said. "And I'm not drinking any more than you guys."

"It's not about drinking or drugs," John said.

"You're letting Isabella control your mind!" Kris yelled.

Nick scowled at him. "You're whacked."

"Nick," Loren said. "I get it. You're into her and you have something and that's cool, but..."

"When was the last time you wrote a song?" Milo interjected.

"Yesterday."

"That wasn't about her?"

Nick furrowed his brow.

"I'm your best friend and you never hang out with me anymore," Kris whined. "What does that tell you?"

"That you're not his best friend." Milo snickered.

"We're happy for you, Nick," John said. "Just don't neglect the band."

"I'm not neglecting the band," Nick argued.

"Denial," Milo declared.

"A girl broke up the Beatles!" Kris barked.

"I'm not letting anyone break up the band," Nick scoffed. "Isabella is different and her band gave us a break."

"We toured with them. They didn't give us a break," Milo said. "Our manager arranged it and it was mutually beneficial."

"Right," Nick said. "Robin arranged it and it was mutually beneficial, so why are you guys tweaking?"

"Just don't let her control you," Loren advised.

"You should talk," Milo said.

"What does that mean?" Loren demanded.

"You guys are all whipped. Kris is right. Girls are breaking up the band," Milo ranted. "George isn't even here half the time now."

"I'm right," Kris said gleefully. "Just me and Milo have our own minds."

"Speak for yourself," Milo said.

"Do you think George is going to leave the band?" John asked with concern.

"George wouldn't do that," Nick said dismissively.

"They're having a kid," Loren said. "That's what broke up my last band."

"George won't leave the band," Nick insisted with irritation. "Are we through here?" He glanced at his phone.

"I could learn to play guitar," Kris said. "I could be a stand-up."

"You mean stand by," John said. "But you couldn't pick it up that fast. George is really good."

"Listen, Nick," Milo said. "We're just worried about the future of the band. Things are happening for us now and you're not writing the type of stuff that got us where we are and George is gone half the time."

"You guys started the band, but now you're both distracted by your personal lives," John pointed out.

"We just want to make sure the band is your priority," Milo said.

"Right." Nick was supposed to be over at Isabella's in half an hour for dinner. He stood up. "The band comes first."

"*Black Ice.*" Milo held up a fist.

"*Black Ice*," everyone responded, raising their fists as well, including Nick.

Then he pulled his keys from his pocket. "Later."

***

Tina wore black maternity pants and a shimmery red top. She ran her hand over her rounded tummy. She felt great other than increased hunger and a little fatigue. She wore her low red heels and had pulled the sides of her white hair back with a sparkly silver barrette.

George had grown out his beard and mustache. It was common here where it kept men's faces warmer. She liked the way he looked. His long dark hair was pulled back into a ponytail, which was usually how he wore it unless he was on stage. Black jeans and a green shirt finished his look.

They climbed the narrow stairway to the event space. The door was propped open, and the room was already milling with elves and others. A buffet was set up on one side of the room with an open bar on the other. Tina wished she could have the Borealis Blizzard specialty drink that was so popular. Next year.

White mini lights lined the walls, and silver streamers hung from the beams. The tables were draped with the usual green and red checkered tablecloths. Poinsettia centerpieces adorned each table along with mini lanterns and mistletoe was strategically dangling around the room. The wide windows revealed a stunning view of the Northern Lights. The vivid colors sprayed across the darkened sky were mostly green and blue, with a hint of purple shimmering at the edges.

"Every time I see this, it takes my breath away," George said. "You're probably used to it."

"Not really. It's a little different every year and now I see it through your eyes." Tina smiled.

George pulled her underneath the mistletoe. "I'll never forget our first kiss."

"I was shocked to see you at the festival that year," Tina remembered. "Lisa surprised me."

"I was pretty surprised myself when I saw this place for the first time. Now here we are a few years later and things have turned out better than I ever imagined." George tilted her chin up. "Do you know how much I love you?"

"As much as I love you." Tina closed her eyes and felt his warm lips meet hers.

"I knew I'd find you under the mistletoe." Lisa approached them.

"The room looks fantastic," Tina enthused.

"I tried to come up with something new this year, but we ended up doing pretty much the same thing." Lisa shrugged. "The fun part is picking out the music and the menu. They have those yummy Borealis Blizzard drinks again." She clamped her hand over her mouth. "Oh, I forgot. You can't drink."

"I know." Tina made a sad face.

"I won't drink either," George said.

"Your parents are sitting with Gerta and Jann next to our table. Kai and Sonia are with them. We have our own table." Lisa pointed. "Grab some food and meet us over there."

"Okay." Tina nodded.

They made their way over and stood in line at the buffet table. Tina breathed in the delectable aroma wafting from the food.

"It smells so good."

"I'm glad they always have vegetarian options," George said. "I hope they have that dessert again. It was really good."

"Powdered Snowball Tortes," Tina said. "Since I can't drink, I'm having two."

The clatter of silverware and the chatter of conversations filled the room. Laughter broke out in spurts as they enjoyed their delicious meal. Santa and Clara caught up with their old friends, Gerta and Jann. After dessert, everyone mingled and Tina circulated, greeting elves and their families and beaming through congratulations. She felt incredibly happy and lucky to have her family and friends gathered together. If only Nick were here.

"I just can't get over the Northern Lights." George wrapped his arms around her from behind, resting his arms on her stomach and his chin on her shoulder as they admired the spectacular display.

"It's beautiful," she murmured.

"You're beautiful," he said. "I understand why this would be hard to give up. I don't want you to quit doing what you were meant to do. I mean it. I know you love it, and I can't blame you."

"Thank you." Tina turned to face him. "And I don't want you to quit the band. That's what you love and besides, Nick would kill me."

"He'd kill both of us. I guess we'll just have to make this work."

"I think we're doing a pretty good job so far."

"It gives us time to miss each other," George said.

Music thumped as tables were pushed aside to make room to dance, and the floor quickly filled up with couples. Tina was delighted to see her mother and father laughing and dancing. She pointed them out to George.

"Someday that will be us. Older, but still having fun," he said.

"With our kids watching."

"And laughing at how uncool we look." He grinned.

Tina put her hand on her tummy, and George placed his hand on top of hers.

"Next year, we'll have a baby," Tina whispered.

***

"I don't know why you and George told his sister," Clara said. "You're telling too many people."

"And doing interviews," Santa griped.

"Everybody thought the interview was just a joke,"

Tina reminded him. "Mom, George wanted to tell Gemma because she kept insisting on visiting us. She won't tell anyone."

But Tina worried she might tell Loren, and then the whole band would find out.

"You said she didn't believe you when you told her," Clara said. "So why not leave it at that?"

"George is close to Gemma, and he wanted to tell her and let her visit. He's part of this family and if he wants to tell his sister, then he can," Tina asserted."

"Okay," Clara said. "Don't get yourself worked up."

"It's too late to do anything about it now," Santa said. "They're here."

The snow taxi had pulled up and George and Gemma were emerging. They each lugged a suitcase up the steep steps.

Gemma's eyes were wide. "This place is real? Am I dreaming?"

George helped her off with her coat and hung it up. "I told you."

"You remember my parents," Tina said.

Gemma stared at Santa, who now had a full white beard and mustache. "You look like... but you can't be. You're thinner."

"I lost weight." Santa patted his belly. "No more milk and cookies."

"Gemma, it's nice to have you," Clara said graciously. "George, please put her stuff in Nick's room."

"I can't believe..." Gemma stammered. "This can't be..."

"I hope you're ready to pitch in," Clara said. "We could use the help. Things always get busier after the festival."

"This is your room," George pointed down the hall. "I'll take you on a tour tomorrow. You'll be able to see the reindeer out the window."

"They don't like strangers," Tina explained. "But we might see them at the pub one night."

"Everybody gets excited about the reindeer," Santa commented to Clara.

"So all the stuff in the article was real?" Gemma asked with disbelief. "I have to be dreaming."

"Classic case of adult denial," Santa said to Clara.

"Why do adults have such a hard time believing?" Clara shook her head.

"I don't know what to say." Gemma's eyes were wide.

"That's unusual for her," George told them.

"Now that you know it's real, I'd appreciate it if you didn't write a book based on the article," Tina said. "There's already an actress who wants to option the rights for a movie."

"I forbid it!" Santa suddenly pounded his fist on the counter, making all of them jump.

"What's this about a movie?" Clara demanded.

"It's not up to me, Mom," Tina said. "I think it's up to the magazine. I'm sorry I didn't tell you sooner. I was hoping nothing would come of it."

"It probably won't happen," George said. "She went back to England to do another movie."

"You have not done a good job of being discreet about who we are." Clara shook her finger at Tina.

"I know. I'm sorry," Tina said contritely. "It just seems to snowball."

"No pun intended." George chuckled.

Gemma shook her head. "I feel like I stepped through the looking glass or went down the rabbit hole or flew over the rainbow. Maybe all three at once."

***

Tina sat at her desk, staring at her computer screen and thinking of baby names.

"I know. How about Georgina if it's a girl?" Lisa asked. "It combines both of your names."

Tina wrinkled her nose. "That's cute, but I want the baby to have his or her own name."

"Yeah. I hear you." Lisa turned back to her computer at the little table right inside the door.

"This is Tina's office," George said, entering with Gemma.

She still had the same wide-eyed look of disbelief she'd had the night before upon her arrival.

"Hi, Gemma," Lisa said.

"Oh, hi." Gemma seemed surprised to see her.

"I'm Tina's assistant." Lisa gave a little laugh. "I know how you feel. I was blown away the first time I came here."

"I just can't believe it," Gemma said. "How does all this exist without anyone knowing?"

"The children know," Tina said.

"Wait till you see the reindeer," Lisa said. "You can see them out the window."

Tina turned and looked out towards the main barn. "They're not outside right now. Maybe later."

"Rudy... I mean, Rudolph likes to do karaoke at the pub," Lisa said.

"Karaoke?" Gemma repeated.

"This place is enchanted or something," Lisa said. "The reindeer talk and the sleigh really flies and, oh, there are talking snowmen. It's wild."

Gemma stared at her.

"I wonder if there are talking snow women too." Lisa frowned.

"Don't be silly," Tina said. "Of course there are."

"There you have it." Lisa turned back to Gemma, who continued to stare at her.

"I think she's in shock," George said. "I've never seen her like this."

Gemma cleared her throat. "I'm fine. I'm just... stunned. I mean, I never imagined... I just didn't think..."

"Why don't you take her on a tour?" Tina suggested.

"Yeah, that's what I was doing," George said. "Can you come with us? I don't know my way around yet."

"Sure." Tina got up from her desk.

They walked all over the enormous building and Tina explained the function of each department. They viewed the warehouse, the toy shop, the IT department, the cafeteria, and the mailroom.

"So, this is the family toy business that's seasonal," Gemma said as they neared Tina's office.

"This is it," Tina answered. They stopped at Walter's office. "You remember Walter. He's the foreman for the United North Pole Workers."

"There's a union for the elves?" Gemma asked incredulously.

"And the reindeer. Not that we need one," Tina answered. "We treat the employees very well and work closely with Walter on any issues."

"That's correct," Walter concurred. "Nice to see you, Gemma."

"You too." Gemma shook her head and looked at Tina. "This is amazing. It's a really impressive place."

"It's a lot of responsibility," George said. "Tina does a great job. She made a lot of improvements after her father retired."

"I just updated some things," Tina said. "He wanted to do things the way they've always been done. We just modified some of the machinery and use more computer programs."

"So, your father is the real deal? He's the real Santa? The one who brought our presents when we were kids?" Gemma glanced at George.

"My father-in-law is Santa." George beamed. "Crazy, huh? But now, Tina is Santa. Or Santina, I should say. I guess my wife is Santa now."

"Santina, like in the article." Gemma gazed at Tina. "Unbelievable. Santa really is a woman now."

"That's me." Tina shrugged.

"She's modest," Walter said. "She's doing a spectacular job. It wasn't easy to jump in after her father. She had big boots to fill, so to speak." He chuckled.

"I couldn't have done it without Walter. And Lisa."

They strolled back to Tina's office.

"How was your tour of the building?" Lisa asked.

"Wow." Gemma shook her head.

"I know, right?"

"This must be such a fun place to work," Gemma said.

"Totally," Lisa answered. "Wait until we take you to the pub. It will blow your mind all over again."

Tina walked back to her desk. "I should've gotten tea while we were downstairs."

"I was going to get coffee, anyway. I'll bring you back some," Lisa said.

Gemma leaned toward her. "Walter. I get it. He's cute."

Lisa smiled. "Anyone else want anything?"

"No, thanks. We'll let you get back to work," George said.

"Oh, some of the reindeer are out." Tina noticed.

Gemma hurried over to the window behind Tina's desk and stood beside her.

"What are they doing?"

"They're just kicking around that ball. They're probably keeping score. They're very competitive."

The rest of the reindeer loped out of the barn.

"That big one is Blitzen," Tina explained. "He's sort of the head reindeer. That one jumping around is Rudolph."

"The one who does karaoke?"

"Yes, that's him."

"Are all the reindeer male?" Gemma asked.

"Some are female."

"I wonder if they ever put their play on," Lisa said. "They were supposed to do it the same night as the festival. I wish I could've seen it."

Gemma shook her head. "I know this is all a crazy dream."

30 *Unbearable*

"Why don't you visit Gerta by yourself?" Tina asked.

"I'll do that some other time," Clara answered. "I want to ask her how you're doing."

"You can do that without me there. I don't feel like getting all bundled up to go out," Tina said. "I just want to sit by the fire and have hot chocolate."

"You can do that at Gerta's," Clara said. "Now get your boots on and let's go."

Tina and Gemma put on their boots and coats and scarves and gloves. Gemma pulled her scarf below her mouth.

"I can't believe how cold it gets here."

"See? She doesn't want to go out," Tina said to Clara.

"It'll be nice for her to see some of the scenery," Clara responded.

"There is no scenery. Everything is white," Tina argued.

"She can ride with you," Clara said decisively.

Tina and Gemma followed her down the steps and into the garage where the snowmobiles were parked.

"What's all that?" Tina pointed to the large bundle strapped to the back of a snowmobile.

"I just packed some stuff I'm bringing to Gerta's," Clara said. "Let's get going. She's expecting us."

Tina started the two-seater snowmobile and Gemma climbed on. They headed out across the vast white landscape. The icy wind bit into the exposed skin on their faces and penetrated layers of clothing, chilling them. Tina navigated bumps in the snow and dunes formed by the wind. Two slowly moving white mounds turned four black eyes their way. Tina lifted an arm to wave, and they each raised a snowy arm to wave back.

"What was that?" Gemma yelled.

"That was Frosty and his wife, Chilly," Tina shouted over her shoulder.

After several miles, she pulled up in front of a stout cottage blanketed with snow. She parked and Gemma jumped off.

"Those snowmen were real?!"

"Snowman and snow woman," Tina said. "Yes, they're real."

Clara pulled up beside them with a spray of soft snow. "Go inside, girls. It's cold."

Sonia opened the door before they could knock. She stepped outside as Tina and Gemma stepped in.

"Let me help you, Clara."

They shed their outer clothing and boots and hurried into the toasty warm house. Tina automatically headed into the kitchen. Gerta stepped away from the pot on the stove.

"Tina! Come here." She pulled Tina into a hug.

"Gerta, this is George's sister, Gemma," Tina said and sat down at the big wooden table.

"Welcome, Gemma." Gerta gave her a big hug as well.

"I have hot chocolate all ready for you, Tina."

Gerta poured the steaming liquid from the pot into a mug and poured a second one for Gemma. She put a bag of mini marshmallows on the table and gave them each a spoon. They warmed their hands on the mugs and blew on the hot chocolate to cool it.

"All ready," Clara called.

"Let us go into the living room," Gerta prompted.

Tina looked quizzically at Gerta as she and Gemma took their mugs and followed her.

"Surprise!" Clara shouted.

Wrapped presents were stacked on the wooden coffee table. A pink and blue centerpiece sprouted curled ribbons and a plate of Tina's favorite cinnamon muffins and other pastries were on a side table. Tina stood there puzzled.

"It's a baby shower," Clara said.

Tina gasped. "Oh, my gosh! That's why you wanted me to come." She turned to Gemma. "Did you know?"

Gemma nodded.

"Oh, this is Sonia," Tina said, recovering her manners. "Gemma is my sister-in-law."

"It is nice to meet you," Sonia said in her soft voice.

"Mom, you're so sneaky," Tina accused with a smile, surveying all the wrapped gifts.

"I went a little nuts at the store, but it's hard not knowing if it's a boy or a girl." Clara shrugged.

"Everyone sit," Gerta coaxed.

"Have you chosen names yet?" Sonia asked.

"We're still working on it," Tina replied.

"There's plenty of time," Clara said.

"You're stopping in Boston on your way to Florida so we can see the baby, aren't you?" Gemma asked.

"Yes. I wonder what Evan will think of his new cousin."

"He's excited. I think he thinks the baby will be old enough to play with," Gemma shared.

There was a knock at the door and Lisa stumbled in. "Sorry I'm late. Were you surprised?"

Tina laughed. "Yes."

"Good. I brought my camera. Open your gifts. Let's see what they are."

"Did you see Frosty and Chilly on the way over?" Gemma asked.

"No. They must've blended in with the landscape," Lisa said. "I've never seen her. I've only seen him at the pub."

"Wouldn't he melt in the pub?" Gemma wondered.

"There's a cold room for them," Tina explained.

"Outsiders," Clara said to Gerta.

Gerta smiled. "Hot chocolate, Lisa?"

"Yes. Thanks. Ooh. Can I have a muffin?"

"Help yourself," Gerta said.

"Have you two met?" Tina asked, looking between Lisa and Gerta.

"Lisa and I came over to plan the shower when you were working," Clara said.

"You're really good at keeping secrets." Tina grinned

at Lisa.

"It wasn't easy." Lisa bit into a cinnamon muffin, holding her hand beneath it to catch crumbs.

"Lisa, get a plate and have a seat," Clara told her.

"Want one?" Lisa asked Tina.

She nodded and Lisa brought over two plates and sat between her and Gemma on the comfortable couch. Clara and Sonia sat on padded chairs, and Gerta returned from the kitchen with a mug for Lisa.

"Stand up," Lisa ordered Tina. "Let me get a picture of your stomach."

Tina stood sideways before the fireplace and pulled her loose top tightly over her tummy.

"How many months are you?" Sonia asked.

"About six," Tina answered.

"Aw, look at her." Clara smiled and clasped her hands together.

"Her health is good," Gerta stated.

"I feel great," Tina said. "So much better than the first few months."

Lisa snapped a few photos. "I can't imagine how it feels."

"I love it." Tina sat back down on the couch. "I love feeling the baby move."

"I don't think I'll ever have kids," Gemma declared. "I love my nephew, Evan, and I'll love this little one, and that's enough for me. I just want to focus on my writing."

"I don't think I'll have kids either," Lisa said. "Walter already has kids and I can hardly handle myself, anyway."

"Not everyone is meant to have children," Gerta said.

"It's a huge commitment." Clara nodded. "Women shouldn't feel obligated to have children."

"Right on, Clara." Gemma raised her mug.

"Tina will be a wonderful mother," Sonia said.

"Thank you," Tina responded. "How are your wedding plans coming along?"

"My family is coming from Geneva and there is so much to do," Sonia replied.

"Sonia is well organized," Gerta said. "Everything will go smoothly."

"I hope so," Sonia said.

"Let's guess when the baby is coming," Lisa suggested. "When's your due date?"

"We figured January 7th," Tina answered, looking at Gerta for confirmation.

"And let's guess the gender," Gemma said. "We have to write it down and see who's closest."

"I will write it down," Gerta offered.

"I'll go first," Clara said. "Both my kids were late, so I think this baby will be late too. I'm going to say..." She squinted at Tina. "January 12th and it will be a girl."

"A girl," Lisa agreed. "On January 8th."

Gemma shook her head. "I think it's going to be a boy on January 10th."

"I'm not playing," Gerta said.

Everyone looked at Sonia. "January 2nd. A boy."

"You think it will come early?" Gemma asked.

Sonia shrugged.

"Hmm. Two guesses for a boy and two for a girl," Lisa said. "Gerta, are you sure you don't want to be the tiebreaker?"

Gerta shook her head.

"So, it could happen anywhere from January 2nd to January 12th," Gemma summarized.

"I'm going to get more marshmallows," Tina said. "I'll be right back."

"Let me pour a little from the pot to warm it up for you." Gerta went into the kitchen with her.

Tina handed her mug to Gerta.

"How are you feeling?"

"Great. Just a little tired sometimes," Tina answered.

"I can feel the storm coming."

Tina's eyes widened. "How close is it? When will it happen?"

"I was afraid it would disrupt the wedding, but it will not come that soon." Gerta handed the mug back.

"When do you think it will happen?" Tina asked again.

"It will happen in December." Gerta nodded. "Yes. December. We shall not upset anyone."

"Presents!" Lisa called out.

Tina dropped some marshmallows into her hot chocolate and followed Gerta back to the living room.

"I will write everything down," Gerta said.

Tina set her mug on the coffee table and sat between Lisa and Gemma. A big storm was coming in December. How bad would it be? What could they do to prepare? She began making a mental list of supplies.

"Tina." Clara was holding out a gift.

"Oh." Tina smiled and tore off the wrapping paper.

One by one Clara handed the gifts to Tina while Lisa took photos. She delighted in the little outfits and blankets and diapers and other items. She held up tiny socks, marveling at how small they were. She paged through a book that her mother had bought to document the baby's milestones. First word. First steps. First tooth. Tina placed her hand on her tummy when she felt a little kick.

"Can I?" Gemma asked.

Tina nodded, and Gemma felt a brief flutter of movement. Her face lit up with a smile.

"Wow," she whispered.

***

"Are you going to miss me, Nicky?" Isabella asked. "I'm leaving in three days." She scooted closer to him and tucked her bare feet beneath her on the couch.

"Hm." He had just taken a bite of pizza.

"Well, are you?" she nudged him.

"Yeah."

"Tell me how much."

Nick looked into her blue or green eyes and became

transfixed. His mouth fell open a bit.

"Tell me, Nicky." Isabella brushed her fingertips along his neck.

"A lot."

She dropped her hand. "For a songwriter, you sure *don't* have a way with words."

"Life will be unbearable without you," he said honestly.

She smiled. "I'll miss you too."

"The guys are jamming me because I'm not writing as much," Nick confessed.

"And I broke all my rules for you," Isabella said softly. "Do you think we're bad for each other?"

"I don't care."

"That's what I like about you."

They each took a bite of pizza.

"This separation will be good," she said, chewing. "We can both focus on our bands. You can write. I can get back into my head. I have to go inward."

"Huh?"

"I have to go to my core. You know," Isabella said. "The center of my being to find the magic."

Nick still didn't know what the heck she was going on about, but he nodded.

"You have a totally different process than I do," she said. "My mother hates you. She thinks we're too different."

"She's whacked."

Isabella laughed. "So, when will I meet your parents?"

"What for?"

"I'm curious."

"I like that you only know me and not my family."

She knew him as Nick, not as a Claus. And that was good, especially after a childhood of living under the burden of that name. Kids were either nice to him because of who his father was or they teased him because of who his father was.

"Come on. Tell me what they're like," Isabella

cajoled.

"My father is really stubborn and grouchy, and my mother is nice," he said. "But she always wants me to do something."

"Like what?"

"I don't know. Go over there and have dinner. Go home and work for the family business. Whatever."

"What was your childhood like?"

"Why?"

"I'm just trying to get to know you better, Nicky."

"Right." He scowled. "My father always pressured me for my whole life to run the family business when he retired. They just wouldn't let it go. I had to get out of there."

"That's why you're so rebellious." Isabella nodded.

"Not." He bristled. "My eyes are just open."

"I like it."

"What?"

"For a song. Open your eyes. It's a good message."

"I need some paper."

Nick wiped his hands on a napkin while Isabella got up and retrieved a pad and pen. He jotted down the words as they came to him.

"I love to see your creative fire," she said.

"Right."

He flipped over the page on the pad and continued writing. Then he threw it down on the coffee table and picked up his pizza.

"Wish I could write a song that fast," she said. "You probably *could* score a whole movie. Have you heard from Skyler?"

"Nah."

"Are you going home for the holidays while I'm gone?" she asked

"I have to go to a wedding up north next month."

"Will you be there for Thanksgiving?"

"Probably."

"Will you miss me?" Isabella smiled flirtatiously.

Nick set down his pizza. "It will be agony."

31 *Winter White*

"I'm so glad I came to visit." Gemma hugged Tina. "It was so nice meeting you." She gave a brief wave to Santa and Clara.

"Remember, not a word to anyone about us or where we are." Clara put a finger to her lips.

"Not a word," Gemma repeated. "And I'm not going to write the book."

"Good," Santa said with a firm nod.

"But I don't understand why you complain that no one believes, yet you don't want anyone to know the truth." Gemma shook her head.

"People should believe here." Santa patted his chest over his heart.

"But we don't want to publicize this place," Clara said.

Gemma nodded. "Tourists would ruin this peaceful little town. You're right."

"Thanks for the stuff for the baby," Tina said. "I love the mobile."

"You're welcome. I can't wait to see that little one. I wonder if the baby will have dark hair or light hair," Gemma said.

"It's going to be a real surprise." Clara drifted off to the kitchen.

Santa turned on the TV.

George hugged Gemma. "Thanks for coming all this way."

"I'm not looking forward to the flight home," she said. "And all Mom and Dad's questions."

George shrugged. "It's just a toy company."

Gemma laughed. "Okay." She pointed a finger at Tina. "So Nick is your brother and he grew up here too. He was supposed to be Santa, wasn't he?"

"What?" Santa looked up.

"We're just talking, Dad," Tina said. "Yes. It was supposed to be Nick, but the family history revealed that the true intention was for Santa..."

"What?" Santa answered.

"We're just talking, Dad," Tina said again. "Anyway, it was always supposed to be a woman. We discovered that only a few years ago."

"Really?" Gemma asked. "I bet your family history is fascinating."

"And you didn't believe us," George teased.

"You called me a nut job," Tina reminded her.

"Did I?" Gemma asked.

"You said the woman in that article was a nut job." Tina smiled.

"And that woman is you." Gemma frowned. "I'm sorry I didn't believe you, but it's just so..."

"Unbelievable," George finished.

Gemma sighed. "Well, you really did blow my mind and now I can't even tell anyone."

"Now you know how I feel," George said.

"And you can't even tell the family who your wife really is and where you go every winter." Gemma shook her head. "That must be hard."

"But it's worth it." George put his arm around Tina and pulled her close.

Gemma smiled. "Thanks for trusting me, even though I didn't believe you at first."

They heard a beep.

"The snow taxi is here," Tina said. She gave Gemma another hug.

"Have a safe trip," George said.

Gemma pulled on her gloves and wrapped the red scarf that Tina had given her around her neck and mouth. George opened the door, and she pulled her suitcase behind her, turning to give them one last wave.

***

Tina hurried out to the main barn before going to her office. George was in the shower and her parents had already gone to work. She wanted to talk to Blitzen before she said anything that would alarm them, though her anxiety level had risen a notch since Gerta's warning at her shower.

Thoughts bounced around in her head as she rushed along the icy path to the barn. In her haste, she slipped, landing on her side.

"Ow!" she cried out as pain shot into her ribs. She pushed herself to a sitting position and put a gloved hand on her belly. "Are you okay? Please be okay."

She felt tears gather in her eyes. She knew teardrops could freeze in this cold, crisp weather.

"Tina!" Dancer trotted toward her. "Are you okay? Grab my leg." Dancer pulled her up. "Come inside."

Tina carefully followed her into the barn and Dancer pulled the door shut. Tina hurried toward the wood stove. She was shaking. She pulled off her glove and stuck her hand in her coat pocket, hoping to find a tissue. There was none. She wiped her eyes with her hand.

"Don't worry," Dancer said. "You're bundled up. The baby is cushioned."

"You think so?" Tina asked hopefully.

"They're pretty well cushioned, anyway."

"But the ground is so hard," Tina fretted.

"Call Gerta if you notice anything different," Dancer advised.

"Okay." Tina pulled off her other glove and held her hands before the fire. "I need to talk to Blitzen."

Dancer rubbed her snout on Tina's arm reassuringly. Tina ran her hands along her long neck and head.

"Thanks, Dancer."

Prancer appeared from behind the wall that separated the front and back sections of the barn.

"Oh, it's Tina."

Blitzen slowly came around and approached them.

"Tina fell on the ice," Dancer reported.

He came closer to Tina and nodded his head low in front of her. He snorted.

"The kid's okay."

"How do you know?" Tina bit her lip.

"Call Gerta if you must," he said. "She'll tell you the same."

"Okay." Tina couldn't help still feeling nervous about it. "She said the storm is coming next month."

"That's right."

"How bad will it be, Blitzen?" Tina asked.

"I sense it will be a big storm, possibly lasting for a few days," he said.

"What can we do?"

"The mayor advised everyone in town to stock up on supplies. That's all we can do."

"But what will happen? Is everyone going to be okay?" Tina pressed.

"I don't know." Blitzen shook his head. "My advice is to stock up and make an emergency plan for the elves to go to the safest place in the building."

Tina nodded. They had already begun gathering provisions. They had generators and lanterns and food and water. She thought quickly. Where was the safest place in the building? Somewhere on the ground floor with few external walls. Unless the entire building collapsed. The warehouse had been rebuilt. Maybe it was sturdier than the rest of the building, but there were stacks of boxes that could topple. They could clear out one side.

"I hope you'll be safe out here," she said to Blitzen.

"We'll be fine," he assured her. "We have a storm cellar below." He stamped his hoof.

"I didn't know that," Tina said.

"It's small, but we can all fit."

Donner kneeled down. "Oi, Tina. Get on. I'm going to take you back. It's cold out here."

"Thanks, Donner."

Tina put her gloves back on and climbed onto his back. She grasped his antlers as he slowly stood up.

"Ready?"

"Yes."

Dancer opened the barn door, and Donner took her back to the building. He lowered himself and she jumped to the ground.

"Thanks, Donner." She gave him a little wave.

He nodded and watched her ascend the steps to the apartment, deep in thought about the preparations.

***

Tina donned the ice-blue dress her mother had bought for her to wear to the wedding. It had a high waist and showed off her rounded tummy. She pulled her hair back with her sparkly silver barrette and stepped into the blue ankle boots with the faux fur lining.

"You look stunning," George said. He wore a light gray suit and a red tie. "Let me put this on you." He held out a necklace.

Tina gasped. "It's beautiful. What's this for?"

"It's for the mother of my child." He grinned.

Tina admired the pale blue gemstone ringed with sparkling Swarovski crystals as he fastened it around her neck.

"It matches my ring," she noticed with delight, holding up her hand. "Thank you." She turned to kiss him.

"The snow taxi's here," Walter called to them.

"I'm liking this." Tina touched George's beard and mustache. "You look like a real North Pole man now."

"Yeah?" He rubbed his chin and chuckled.

Tina opened the bedroom door as Lisa came out of the bathroom. She wore a flattering silver dress. Walter had on a bluish-gray suit with a royal blue tie. They pulled on their coats and piled into the snow taxi. It was traditional for everyone to wear light colors, with bold ties for the men. Parents of the bride and groom wore darker colors, and the bride and groom wore off-white.

Clara and Santa had left earlier with Nick, who had only arrived the day before and was probably still sleep deprived. He had mostly slept since his arrival and they hadn't had much chance to visit yet, though George was especially happy to see him.

Butterflies surged in Tina's stomach. She stared out the window at the blur of whiteness whizzing by. It wasn't every day you watched your ex-boyfriend get married. A part of her still felt connected to Kai. She probably always would. They'd known each other since they were little kids and would always know each other. Their parents were friends and her brother was friends with Kai. And she'd always believed that he would be the one she'd marry.

In a strange way, she felt like they were part of each other. A piece of her heart would always belong to him. But her true love sat beside her, and she had no regrets. She turned and gazed at George, who was talking to Walter. Again, she reflected on how lucky she was. Lisa caught her eye, and they smiled at each other.

The venue was large, with a low ceiling that made it feel more intimate. Everything was white or off-white. Ice sculptures were interspersed amongst the round tables. The bride and groom would sit at the middle table with both sets of parents. All the other tables radiated out around them. The tall, slender silver vase centerpieces held white flowers and a chilled bottle of champagne was atop each table. The wedding would be performed at the stage on one side of the room while the guests sat at the tables where they would later eat. The space in front of the stage would be used as a dance floor after the ceremony.

They found the table where Nick was sitting. Clara and Santa were at the next table.

"You look fat," Nick said to Tina.

"I'm not fat. I'm pregnant," she said indignantly.

"Your stomach is like Dad's used to be." He guffawed.

"Hey, quit insulting my wife." George punched his arm.

"Don't listen to him. You look great," Lisa said,

seating herself. She leaned over and said in a low voice, "Are you okay?"

Tina pulled out the chair beside Lisa and sat down while George and Walter stood and talked with Nick. "It's a little weird."

"Being at your ex's wedding." Lisa nodded. "Hold on. Is that a new necklace?"

"George just gave it to me." Tina touched it. "It matches my ring."

"It's exquisite."

Soft music played, and everyone settled into their seats. Kai and Sonia entered from opposite sides of the room at the same time and ascended the steps to the empty stage with a backdrop of white drapes. Tina's heart jumped a little when she saw Kai in his cream-colored suit and white tie. Sonia's dress was lacy and hung straight down to her ankles. She wore a headdress trailing ribbons down her back. They faced each other and joined hands.

Tina's mind wandered as they recited their written vows to each other, promising loyalty, forgiveness, and honesty. She remembered when they were little, playing in the toy shop with Nick. She couldn't recall a time when he hadn't hovered in her life except for when he'd run off to Geneva after high school and broken her heart. She felt a tear roll down her cheek as she rose to her feet with the other guests to applaud the newly married couple.

Kai and Sonia descended the front steps to their table and poured glasses of champagne. Then they circulated clockwise, visiting each table to be toasted and congratulated.

Tina stood again when Kai approached. She reached out her arms, and he bent down to embrace her.

"I'm so happy for you," she whispered, not able to stop her tears.

"We are all of us family," he said to her.

He released her, and George shook his hand while

she hugged Sonia.

"You look radiant," Tina told her.

"You too," she demurred.

After Kai and Sonia had circled the room, the music grew louder. Some people danced and others mingled. Kai led Sonia onto the dance floor and they slowly swayed, holding each other.

George took Tina's hand and smiled at her. "They look happy."

"Yes." She dabbed her eyes with a napkin.

"It's okay," he said.

"What?"

"Whatever you're feeling." He glanced at the dance floor and back at her.

"Everything is the way it should be," Tina said. "They're perfect together."

"So are we." He kissed her hand.

"George, you know pregnant women are more emotional, right?" Lisa asked. "It's all the hormones."

He smiled. "Thanks, Lisa."

"So, why wasn't there a minister or justice of the peace or something?" she asked.

"It's not necessary," Walter said. "They have all these witnesses and they sign something that makes it legal."

"That's it?"

"That's it," he said.

"I always thought you and Kai were going to get married," Nick said to Tina.

Clara hit his shoulder from behind. She turned in her seat and glared at him.

"Ow! Why does everybody keep hitting me?" he groaned.

"Tina and Kai broke up years ago," Clara said. "That's in the past."

"I don't know about anybody else, but I'm going to check out the buffet table." Lisa pushed back her chair. "Come with me, Walter."

George pulled Tina up and kissed her. "Let's go feed

the baby."

Tina smiled. "That's a good idea."

***

Tina shuffled out of the bedroom in her pink bathrobe and matching fuzzy slippers and yawned.

"I thought *I* was a late sleeper," Nick said.

He and George sat at the small dining table drinking coffee.

"I'm sleeping for two," she replied, sitting next to George and resting her head on his shoulder.

"Let me get you some juice and then I'll warm up your oatmeal," he said.

"Okay." She yawned again while he went into the kitchen. "Where are Mom and Dad?"

"They went to work," Nick said. "They're into it like maniacs and they want me to help in the mailroom. They think I'll get all sentimental or something."

"I enjoy reading the letters."

George returned and set a glass of orange juice before her. "I enjoy helping, too."

"You don't have to try to impress the in-laws anymore," Nick said.

George shook his head. "Why are you so down on this place? It's cool. No pun intended."

"Not."

Tina took a sip of juice. "How's Isabella? How is that going?"

"It's intense," he told them. "She has this power over me like a spell or something."

"You're in love," George said. "That's what that is."

Nick furrowed his brow. "No, it's like she bewitched me."

George laughed as he returned to the kitchen.

"Seriously," Nick insisted. "She does magic or something on me. It's wild."

"Sounds like love," Tina said.

"How's the band?" George called.

"They don't get it. They said I don't write enough anymore. They tried to do an intermission on me. Wait... what's it called?"

"Intervention?" Tina asked.

"Right."

"Have you been writing?" George asked. He placed a bowl in front of Tina.

"I just wrote a song called 'Eyes Open.' I don't know what they're tweaking about," he said. "But they're bugging about you, too."

"Me? What about me?"

"They think you're going to quit the band."

George and Tina exchanged looks before he turned back to Nick. "They said that?"

"They said you're gone half the time already."

"I'm not missing anything important, am I?" George asked. "It's only a few months a year except this year because of the baby."

"Don't sweat it." Nick waved his hand.

"I don't want to mess up anything with the band," George said. "Nick, you know I won't let you down."

"George isn't quitting the band," Tina said adamantly. "We'll be back down in January after the baby's born."

"Is that why you're so fat like Dad was?" Nick chuckled.

"Nick! That isn't funny!" Tina yelled.

32 *More Gravy*

"I'm glad we're all together today," Clara said as they gathered in the cafeteria. "It's been a few years since the entire family was together for Thanksgiving."

All the elves had gone home for the holiday, and Clara and George had taken over the kitchen to prepare their meal. They pushed a few tables together and everyone helped bring the food from the cafeteria kitchen.

"Where's the beer?" Nick asked.

"No alcohol," Clara responded. "Your sister is pregnant."

"So we all can't drink?" he protested. "What kind of party is this?"

"It's not a party. It's a family dinner," Santa said sternly.

"How am I supposed to get through this sober?" he asked George.

George grinned and handed him a bottle. "Here. Put this on the table."

"What is it?" Nick squinted at the label. "Sparkling cider? Isn't there something with alcohol around here?"

"Nick," Clara said in a warning tone.

"Right."

Tina set the table with plates and silverware. She looked up as Nick approached.

"I'm so glad you stayed for Thanksgiving. I think the last time we were all together was up here before I took over."

"Right."

"So much has happened in the last few years and next year we'll have one more at the table."

"Who?" he asked.

"The baby."

"Right."

"We're still trying to decide on names," she said. "Can you believe all the great things that have happened in the last few years? I got married and started running the business and things are happening with the band. Soon you'll be headlining your own tour."

"Right." He poured himself a glass of cider.

Clara set the Tofurkey on the table. "Nick, wait until we toast."

"I'm thirsty." He took a sip.

"We have a large group this year." Clara put her hands on her hips. "We made plenty of food, though, and George made some pecan pies. I can't wait to try a piece."

"Really, Nick," Tina continued. "I'm so proud of you. You did what you wanted to do. *Black Ice* is very successful."

"Right."

"I wish Isabella could be here," she said.

"Now, don't you tell her who we are," Clara cautioned him.

Nick rolled his eyes. "Don't worry. I won't broadcast it like Tina."

"Nick!" Tina pushed his shoulder. "Be nice to me."

Lisa brought a platter of food to the table. "I feel like a server in a restaurant. How do they carry everything?"

Walter set two baskets of rolls on the table. "Everything smells so good."

"I'm hungry," Tina said. "I can't wait to eat."

"Eating for two," Lisa said. "You look like you're ready to pop."

"I hate that expression." Tina scrunched up her nose.

"I should've picked a date sooner than January 8th for my guess," Lisa said. "Like tomorrow."

"No way. I'm not due for another six weeks," Tina objected.

"She'll be late," Clara said confidently. "I was late both times."

George pulled out Tina's chair. "Do you need anything?"

"No, thanks." She tilted her head up to receive his

kiss.

"See what I have to put up with all the time?" Lisa nudged Nick and he grimaced.

There was the scraping of chairs as everyone seated themselves. Tina placed her napkin on her lap. She felt so happy that all her loved ones were together and especially happy that Nick was there with them.

"Now, before we eat, let's do a toast and give thanks for all we have." Clara poured cider into a glass and passed the bottle down. "It just seems as if we don't get together very often anymore. It's nice to have George as part of our family now, and next year we'll have someone new with us."

"Who?" Nick asked again.

"The baby," George answered with a smile.

"We invited your Uncle Kris and Aunt Kandi and, of course, cousin Kris, but they're spending today with her family," Clara said. "And we're happy that Walter and Lisa joined us today. They're a welcome part of this family." She raised her glass. "We're thankful for this meal and all of us here today."

"Amen." Santa held up his glass.

"Don't we still have some beer upstairs?" Nick asked.

"Not now, Nick," Clara said.

Everyone raised their glasses and took a sip of sparkling cider.

"I'm doing a beer run upstairs. Anyone?" Nick scanned the faces around the table.

"You heard your mother. Stay where you are and eat your dinner," Santa ordered.

"Nick, you can have a beer later and you can go to the pub tomorrow," Clara said. "But right now you're having dinner with the family. Be thankful."

"I'm thankful I don't have to babysit Kris. That gets old," Nick muttered.

"You're not babysitting him," Clara said. "You gave him a job as a roadie and your assistant or whatever you have him doing. It was very nice of you to help your cousin out.”

“Kris is okay,” George said, passing the mashed potatoes to Tina.

“That’s easy to say when he doesn’t stick to you like tape,” Nick scoffed.

“Pass that casserole thing, please,” Lisa asked.

“It’s mixed veggies with nut cheese sauce,” George told her. “I usually make it with potatoes, but we’re already having mashed potatoes.”

“Your casseroles are sick,” Nick said to George.

“Nick, apologize to George. His cooking is wonderful,” Clara reproached.

“Mom, that means they’re good,” Tina explained.

“It does?” She frowned. “That doesn’t sound like a compliment.”

“I hope you made a lot of gravy,” Santa said. “Pass it this way.”

“I like a lot of gravy too,” Nick said. “Is there more?”

“There’s more gravy,” George assured them.

Nick pulled out his phone.

“Not at the table,” Clara admonished.

Nick ignored her while he texted.

“Not at the table!” Santa pounded his fist and startled everyone.

“Dad.” Tina reached over and put her hand on his arm. “You’re getting cell service, Nick?”

“Huh?” He put his phone back in his pocket.

“We can’t always get service here,” George said.

“Where *is* Isabella?” Tina asked.

“Not sure.”

Tina felt a little fist or foot poke her rounded tummy. “Oh.”

“Are you okay?” Clara asked anxiously.

“It was just a kick,” Tina said.

“Thank goodness.” Clara took a deep breath.

“Tell that kid not to come during dinner,” Nick said.

“I can’t tell it when to come,” Tina responded.

“It’s going to be early,” Lisa said.

“It’s going to be late,” Clara insisted.

"It's going to be a spoiled brat," Nick said.

"It's okay, Mom." Tina held up her hand before her mother could react. "You're going to love this little baby, Nick. You're going to be the best uncle."

"Uncle Nick." George grinned.

"Are we on schedule?" Santa asked Tina.

"No business at the table," Clara warned.

"Yes, Dad," Tina answered, stealing a glance at her mother.

"Oh, I forgot to mention that Donner hurt his leg playing kickball," Walter said.

"Is he okay?" Lisa took a napkin and wiped gravy from Walter's chin.

"He's got it wrapped. He'll be fine." Walter smiled at Lisa and she gave him a quick kiss.

"We need more gravy," Santa announced.

***

"I can't deal with my parents sober." Nick took a gulp of beer.

"I used to feel that way about your father," Walter admitted.

"They're not so bad." George signaled the bartender.

"You didn't have to grow up with them," Nick grumbled.

"They couldn't have been that bad," George said.

"Walter, you were there," Nick said. "I rest my witness."

"Have you heard from Isabella?" George asked.

"Nah. She's in Europe somewhere."

"What about Skyler?" George wondered.

"She's in England making some whacked movie," Nick answered.

"How are things with you and Lisa?" George turned to Walter. "You look happy."

"Things are better since we had the house renovated," Walter said. "I didn't understand how claustrophobic she felt."

"You've been together a few years now," George noted.

"I know. I never expected to get into another serious relationship, but then Lisa happened," Walter smiled. "Sometimes I think it'll never last because we're different in so many ways, but somehow it works."

"As long as you're happy," George said.

"Never a dull moment with Lisa. That's for sure." Walter nodded. "What about you and Isabella?" He addressed Nick.

"What about it?" Nick asked.

"Seems pretty serious," Walter said.

"I fall into her eyes and have no will of my own. It's unbearable to be apart." Nick lifted his beer bottle.

Walter and George looked at each other.

"That was poetic," George commented.

"He's in love," Walter said.

"Three more beers." Nick signaled the bartender. "I've lost it with her. There's nobody like her."

"Does she feel the same?" Walter asked.

"She says I understand her and we're electric on stage."

"That you are." George finished his beer.

"She said we're like magnets because we're opposites," Nick shared.

"Magnets," Walter mused. "I like that. Lisa and I are opposites, too."

"Then you get it." Nick clinked beer bottles with him.

"And you're about to be a father," Walter said to George.

"Where are your kids?" George asked.

"They spend a lot of time with my ex in Boulder, Colorado. Sometimes they come here and work in the mailroom."

"That must be tough sometimes," George said sympathetically.

Walter shrugged. "They're not little kids anymore."

"Your kids are cool," Nick said. "We used to play

together."

"That's right," Walter said. "Until my ex moved to Boulder with them when they were teenagers."

"That sucks," Nick said.

"We worked out visitation, but they're grown now," Walter said. "We keep in touch."

"I can't imagine going through that." George shook his head.

"You and Tina will never get divorced," Nick said.

"I hope not," George answered. "She's the love of my life."

"You're the love of *her* life." Nick pointed at him.

"You think?"

"What do you mean?" Nick scrunched his forehead.

"She got emotional at the wedding," George said. "Everyone always thought they'd get married."

"Kai?" Nick shook his head. "That was forever ago."

"It doesn't compare." Walter agreed. "Women get emotional when they're pregnant. It's the hormones."

"Yeah?" George took a sip of beer.

"It's a fact," Walter said. "Tina's crazy about you. How could you doubt that?"

"She's head over feet," Nick stated.

"You always mix up your metaphors." Walter chuckled.

"My meta what?"

"We know what you mean," George said. "Too bad you have to leave the day after tomorrow."

"Got some gigs coming up."

"Are you guys okay covering the local gigs till I get back?" George asked. "I figured it wouldn't be a big deal."

"Right."

"I'll be back after the baby's born in time for our next tour, but I won't be able to make it for our New Year's Eve gig. Are you okay with that?"

Nick nodded. "It's cool. I mean, it's cool."

"I think I've had too much to drink." Walter frowned. "I'm hearing double."

"Tina can't drink. I miss her," George said.

"I miss Lisa," Walter declared.

"You whiners," Nick said. "You get to go home to them. I'm a million miles away from Isabella."

33 *Big Scary Storm*

Tina awoke to the sound of the wind. It could often be heard whipping over the immense open landscape as it sculpted the snow into bumps and dunes. But this sound was different. It was a low, plaintive wail that sounded like an animal. She listened for a few minutes as the sound rose in urgency and pitch and faded before beginning again. Gerta and Blitzen had said the storm would hit in December. It was less than a week before Christmas. She'd been expecting it every morning and thankful when each day had safely passed. Could this finally be it? Was this the big storm that happened every fifty years or so and threatened to decimate the North Pole? She listened until it rattled the windows.

"George," she whispered urgently. "Wake up."

"Hmm."

"George. Wake up." She nudged him.

"Huh?" He opened his eyes.

"Listen."

The wind howled mournfully.

"What is that?" he asked.

"The wind."

"It's really blowing out there."

"Do you think it's the big storm?"

"I don't know."

George got up and padded to the window. Tina stepped into her slippers and stood next to him in front of the window, peering out into the darkness illuminated by the lights by the barns. The red ball that the reindeer played with danced wildly above the ground in the wind. It was mesmerizing. She stared at it, transfixed, until the barn door flew off and rolled along the ground.

"Oh, my gosh!" Tina hurried into the hall and banged on her parents' bedroom door. "Mom! Dad! Wake up!"

"What's happening?" Clara called. "Is it the baby?"

"Get up! It's the storm!" Tina yelled and ran back to the bedroom.

George was getting dressed. "Should we go down to the warehouse?"

"Yes. All the provisions are there." Tina quickly dressed and glanced around the bedroom, trying to determine what to bring. "My necklace." She put it around her neck. "Let's grab our coats and boots. It'll be cold in the warehouse," she said to George.

Tina ran out into the hall, right into Clara.

"Where's Dad?"

"He's in the bathroom," Clara said. "Do you have flashlights?"

"I'll get them," George said.

"We should unplug all the appliances in case there's a power surge," Tina said.

"I got it." George headed for the kitchen.

Tina unplugged the TV and lamps. Everyone donned their coats and pulled on their boots. They scurried down the hall and down two flights of stairs to the other side of the building and into the enormous warehouse. Tina flipped on the overhead lights. One side had been cleared and blankets and pillows were piled in a corner.

"I hope Lisa and Walter are okay," Tina worried.

"And the elves and everyone in town," Santa added.

"I don't hear anything," George said, standing still to listen.

"I wish we could see outside." Tina looked up at the row of windows along the back wall just below the ceiling.

"Maybe it was just some wind," Clara suggested.

"The barn door blew off," Tina told her.

"Well, it could just be a strong wind," Clara said.

Tina paced. Everything was still and quiet. She realized she could hear the ticking of a clock and squinted up at the big round one on the wall. It was almost 3:30 in the morning.

"I'm going to go check things out," Santa said. "It

may have passed."

"I'll go with you," George offered.

Their footsteps echoed as they walked over to the door at the back of the building beneath the windows.

"Come sit down, Tina." Clara patted the stack of blankets beside her. "Don't get yourself worked up."

"I'm just worried about the baby," Tina said.

"There's nothing to worry about."

"I fell the other day. I slipped on the ice," Tina said.

"Did you hurt yourself? Did you talk to Gerta about it?"

"I talked to her on the phone. She thinks everything is okay."

"Then you and the baby are fine." Clara smiled reassuringly.

"I'm glad you're here, Mom," Tina said.

Sometimes it was comforting to have her mother around. They sat watching Santa and George carefully peek out the back door.

"We can go back upstairs," Santa called. "The wind has stopped."

Tina yawned. George jogged back and took her hand to pull her up. "Let's go back upstairs and get into our warm bed."

"I'm glad it was a false alarm," Tina said.

***

Tina stood before her office window and observed the reindeer and a team of elves attempting to reattach the battered barn door. The red ball sat in the snow and Dasher kicked it inside. At this time of year, daylight resembled dusk most of the day.

"That was scary last night," Lisa said. "Our windows shook so much I thought they would shatter."

"If that was the storm, then we got lucky," Tina said. "It wasn't bad at all."

"Walter wanted to cover the windows with these plywood boards, but then it would be like we're in a cave," Lisa said.

Walter leaned against the doorway to Tina's office, holding a mug of coffee. "I should've done it already. I'll just put them on the side of the house that gets the most wind in case we get another storm. It always blows in the same direction."

"You're so smart." Lisa smiled.

"I'm going down to the warehouse to check on supplies. We need more chairs down there," he said. "Want to come?"

"Okay." Lisa lagged behind him. "I hope that was the big scary storm, but it's probably good to be prepared."

Tina seated herself at her desk and tried to focus on her computer. She put her hand on her tummy.

"It's okay, little baby. Don't worry."

Lisa brought her tea when she returned. "Walter thought we should put a fire extinguisher in the warehouse because it burned down during the last big storm."

"Don't we already have one in the warehouse?" Tina asked.

"We didn't see it anywhere and had to take one from the kitchen. The staff didn't like that."

"Let's buy a few more," Tina said. "We need one on each floor and in every department. This building is so big."

"I'll check on how many we have and how old they are. Then I'll do a purchase order." Lisa sat at her computer by the door. "Do you need one for the apartment?"

"I think we have one, but let's get another one."

Walter entered. "I just thought of something."

They both looked up questioningly from their computers.

"Your Santa suit," he said. "It won't fit over your stomach since I altered it."

Tina looked down at her protruding tummy.

"It's a little loose. It might still fit," Lisa said

hopefully.

"I doubt it." Walter rubbed his bearded chin. "I can let it out a little."

"Is there enough time to do that?" Tina asked.

"Sure. I just have to see it on you and figure out how much to let out," he said. "Then I'll bring the pants and jacket home and alter them on my sewing machine."

"I'm glad you thought of that," Tina said. "Thanks, Walter. I appreciate it."

"Not a problem." He shrugged and returned to his office.

"Isn't he great?" Lisa beamed.

"Yes, Walter is great."

"I didn't get enough sleep last night." Lisa yawned. "That stupid wind kept me awake. I'm glad it wasn't worse, though..."

Suddenly there was a loud boom, and the room turned dark. The battery-operated clock ticked on the wall. Tina could make out that it was 10:20 by the dim bit of daylight coming through the window.

"What just happened?" Lisa asked in alarm.

"I don't know." Tina rose from her desk and looked out the window.

The sky had darkened and gusts whipped along the ground, rising up and spraying snow on the window. The reattached barn door flapped like a sheet on a clothesline. Two of the reindeer struggled to pull it closed and fasten it.

"I think the wind is back," Tina said. "Do we have a flashlight?"

Walter ran in, shining a beam into the room. "I think a transformer blew. The backup generators should come on, but we have to get down to the warehouse."

"We need to let everyone know," Tina said. "Let's call each department..."

"That will take too long," he said. "We can use the P.A."

"We have a P.A.?" Tina asked.

"If it still works." He nodded.

"Okay. How does it work?"

He pointed to a button on her phone. "Just lift the receiver and press that button. Hang up when you're finished."

"You mean the button that says 'P.A.'?" Tina shook her head at herself.

Lisa giggled.

The lights flickered and then came back on. The windows rattled threateningly and they could hear the deep moan of the wind.

"That's so eerie." Lisa shivered.

Tina lifted the receiver. "Attention, everyone. The storm seems to be back. Please go directly to the warehouse for safety. Attention, everyone. Please go directly to the warehouse." She hung up.

"Let's go," Walter said.

"George." Tina picked up the phone, but this time there was only crackling. "The phones are out. I need to go to the apartment and get George. If he's even there. He could be helping out somewhere."

The lights flickered in warning.

"I'll get George. You and Lisa go," Walter said. "Take the flashlight."

"Don't we have another flashlight?" Lisa asked frantically.

"I'll go, Walter," Tina insisted. "You and Lisa..."

"No." Walter started toward the door. "You and Lisa go down..."

"I'm your boss, Walter, and I'm telling you..."

"I can run faster than you, Tina."

"That's true," Lisa said. "You just waddle now."

"I do *not* waddle," Tina said indignantly.

"Tina!" They heard George's voice.

Tina rushed out of her office and saw George running down the hallway toward them. He caught up with them and took a moment to catch his breath.

"I was going to do the laundry and had the TV on and they interrupted the show to warn everyone," he said breathlessly. "The storm started in town and is coming this way. It's worse than this morning. We have to get down to the warehouse."

The lights flickered again. They hurried to the stairwell, where they encountered a surge of elves descending to the bottom floor.

"I wonder why the generators won't stay on," Walter mused.

"I unplugged all the appliances again," George told Tina.

"I should've asked everyone to unplug everything," she said.

"We went offline and told everyone to disconnect everything," Ken, head of the IT department, informed her on the stairs.

"Thanks, Ken," Tina said.

"That's good. We don't want to put a strain on the generators," Walter said as they descended.

Once inside the warehouse, they could hear gales raging outside. The very walls seemed to shake, and Tina hoped everyone would be safe. She placed her hand protectively over her stomach.

"Tina!" Clara rushed over to embrace her.

"You used the P.A.," Santa said.

"I didn't even know we had one," Tina said. "Walter showed it to me."

"We hardly ever used that thing." Clara waved her hand. "Your father didn't like it."

"We never had an emergency like this," he said.

"Lisa, help me find the department leads," Tina instructed. "I want to make sure everyone is accounted for."

"You got it." Lisa headed off into the milling crowd.

"I'll find the radio," Walter offered. "I know we have one in here somewhere."

But there was nothing but static to be heard as they huddled together. Everyone had been accounted for, and there was the murmur of anxious voices.

"I hope my house is okay," Rusty worried and others

muttered in agreement, each concerned about their own homes.

"I hope the reindeer are okay," Lisa said.

"They have a storm cellar," Tina said.

"They do?"

"Yes, they do," Walter confirmed.

"That's right," Clara recalled. "Remember when we built the big barn and put that in, dear?" She touched Santa's arm.

"Hmm."

"Your father didn't want to spend the money," Clara revealed to Tina. "But Blitzen insisted on it."

"It was very expensive," Santa said defensively. "They could've come into the warehouse with everyone else."

"Well, I'm glad they have it," Clara said. "We should've built one for ourselves."

"It would've been too expensive to build one big enough for all of us," Santa reasoned. "Look at how many of us there are here."

A loud crack seemed to come from above them. Everyone looked up at the high ceiling, but there was nothing to see. They had only turned on one set of lights, and half the warehouse was in shadow. Some elves had spread blankets and pillows on the floor and settled in. George slid over a chair and pulled Tina onto his lap. Lisa and Walter sat on a folded blanket while he played with the radio dial, hoping to find some news. Clara and Santa perched in chairs.

The wind continued to wail and pound against the building. The upper windows shook with the fury.

George wrapped his arms protectively around Tina. "You're safe," he whispered in her ear.

The baby jabbed Tina in the ribs. "Oh." She clutched her tummy.

"Are you okay?" Clara jumped up.

"It's just a kick, Mom."

"Tina, I really want you to consider letting your father do the delivery on Christmas Eve this year," Clara said firmly. "He's perfectly capable of taking the sleigh out and delivering all the presents."

"So am I," Tina maintained.

"What did Gerta say?" Clara put her hands on her hips.

"She said it's up to me and to listen to my body," Tina answered. "Besides, the suit won't fit Dad anymore. It's been altered."

"Well, it won't fit you either now."

"I'm going to let it out a little," Walter said.

"Then your father will just wear the spare suit," Clara said to Tina.

"What spare suit?" she asked.

"Of course, there's more than one. I'm just not sure where it is. I'll have to look for it." She turned to Santa. "Do you remember where we put it, dear?"

Santa shrugged. "I forgot all about it."

"I bet it's in the back of our closet," Clara said.

"Mom, we don't need it. I'm doing the delivery," Tina stated. "There's no reason..."

Just then, the back door broke off the hinges and came hurtling toward them. George turned his back to it to guard Tina and everyone scrambled. It crashed into the metal shelves along one side of the warehouse with a loud clang before crashing to the floor. Nobody was hurt, but it had given entry to gusts that swept into the room with a roar. Snow dusted the floor and swirled wildly in the air.

Tina jumped up and scanned the room for something to block the opening. She spotted a folding table leaning against some boxes.

"Get the table!" she yelled, pointing. "Stand it on its end and put it against the doorway! Then we'll pile boxes in front of it."

George was the first to reach the table. Some elves assisted him and they carried it toward the doorway, pushing against the wind that pelted them with snow. Lisa and Clara ran over to help.

"Boxes!" Tina shouted.

Santa and George helped stabilize the table while elves stacked heavy boxes against it. George, Santa, Ken and the taller elves placed boxes on top of the stacks and continued piling boxes in front of the table.

"That should hold it," Santa declared.

Tina stared at the dented metal door on the floor. "We might have to order a new door."

"I'll do a purchase order," Lisa said.

"We might still be able to use this one." Walter went over to assess it. "It's dented, but we can probably get it on the hinges."

"We still can't get anything on the radio." Lisa twisted the dial.

Tina settled back on George's lap. Everyone huddled to wait out the storm while the wind raged ferociously outside. They could hear it whipping around the building and threatening havoc.

34 *Family Photos*

The storm lasted for over seven harrowing hours and then tapered off. There were a few broken windows and the barn door had flown off again. A corner section of the roof had peeled off and been flung over 100 feet away from the building. Fritz was found covered in snow in his snow taxi, but he was all right. Now there were drifts as tall as houses that looked like mini mountains along the horizon. Thankfully, there had been no loss of life. The windows had blown out and there had been roof damage to many homes. One roof had come off entirely, but the family had not been home at the time. It took a few days for the power to be restored, and Tina was glad their generators were working. There was no time to waste in these last days before delivery on Christmas Eve.

"I put a drawstring waist on the pants and made slits on the side seams of the jacket to give you some room." Walter set the folded red suit on Tina's desk in her office. "I had to wait until the power was back on to use my sewing machine."

"Great. Thanks, Walter," Tina said.

"Just let me know if it fits."

"I will. Did your broken window get fixed yet?"

"Not yet. I covered it with plywood until they can get out to replace it," he said. "We're on a waiting list."

"I'm glad your house didn't get too much damage."

"It could've been a lot worse," Lisa said from her makeshift desk. "I should've let Walter put those boards up on the windows when he wanted to."

"Are we going to be ready for delivery?" Walter asked. "That storm set us back."

"It'll be close." Tina bit her lip. "Some elves had to go home and deal with the damage to their houses and everyone else is working longer shifts."

"The United North Pole Workers union contract allows for longer shifts this time of year." Walter nodded.

"They started loading the sleigh," Lisa reported. "But not everything is ready."

Tina lifted the landline receiver and pressed the P.A. button. "Attention, everyone. I just wanted to say that I appreciate all of your hard work. I know some of you had damage to your homes, but we're all here for the children and I appreciate your dedication. Thank you so much." She hung up. "I like that. I may have to do that more often."

Clara came into the office. "I found it."

"Found what?" Tina asked.

"I found the extra suit. It was in the storage closet in my workout room. So if you decide…"

"Mom, please quit bugging me about that," Tina groaned. "I'm doing the delivery." Her eyes suddenly widened, and she gripped her stomach.

"Yeah, you are," Lisa said. "I knew I should've changed my bet."

"Oh, my gosh! I don't think that was a kick." Tina stood hunched over, resting one hand on her desk. "This can't be happening now."

"I could tell by the look in your eyes," Lisa said.

"How would you know?" Walter asked. "You've never had a baby."

"I had to deliver my niece because we couldn't make it to the hospital," Lisa explained. "Don't worry, Tina. I'm a professional."

"Call Gerta!" Clara ordered, pointing at her.

"I have to get to the apartment," Tina said.

"Sit down," Walter demanded. "I'll push you."

"We have to time it," Clara said. "Let me know when you feel another one."

"Hold on, Tina."

Walter placed his hands on the back of her chair. She gripped the armrests and held her feet up, and he pushed her toward the doorway.

Lisa picked up the landline on Tina's desk. "What's Gerta's number?"

Clara took the phone. She quickly dialed the number.

"Jann? Tell Gerta to get over here right away. Tina's having... oh, okay." She hung up. "She's already on her way. She knew."

"How does she do that?" Lisa wondered.

"Somehow she always..."

"Mom!" Tina shrieked as Walter pushed her quickly down the hall.

"I'm coming!" Clara ran out of the office with Lisa behind her.

George opened the door at the far end of the hall. "Gerta's here."

Walter wheeled her into the apartment.

"Everyone be calm," Gerta said firmly. "The first baby can take hours. Walter, go tell Santa, but you two keep working. You have a deadline. We will keep you informed. You too, Lisa."

"But I want to be here," Lisa protested.

"Call or come back in a few hours. You have work to do." Gerta helped Tina out of the chair. "George and I set up the bed. We put a plastic garbage bag on top of the sheet with towels covering it to protect the bed and a bunch of pillows, so you will be comfortable."

"Come on," Walter said to Lisa. He pulled the desk chair behind him.

"Give me a ride back to your office," Lisa cajoled.

"Okay. Sit down." He pushed her out into the hall and closed the door behind them.

"Clara, get a pen and paper and keep track of Tina's labor," Gerta instructed.

"What can I do?" George asked.

"Help Tina put on a nightgown and get into bed. Make sure she is comfortable," Gerta said.

"I'm scared," Tina admitted. She had begun to tremble.

Gerta smiled. "I know."

"But why is it early? Is it okay?" Tina fretted.

"Calculations are not always perfect. Babies come

when they are ready."

"It's going to hurt." Tina bit her lip.

"Yes, it will. But you are stronger than you think, and tonight you will have your beautiful baby." Somehow Gerta's calm manner was reassuring.

"I'm here, Tina," Clara said.

"Me too." George helped her into the bedroom. "I won't leave you. I'll be right here."

***

George held Tina's hand while Clara hovered on her other side. Lisa held her camera ready, and Santa and Walter paced in the living room. It had been hours and Tina was exhausted.

"One more push," Gerta encouraged. "Just one more will do it."

Tina shut her eyes, held her breath, and pushed as hard as she could. And then she heard a little whimper. And then it grew louder.

"You did it," George murmured in her ear. "We have a baby."

Tina's tears flowed. George cried. Clara cried. Lisa cried.

"It is a girl," Gerta announced. "A little girl."

Lisa ran out to the living room. "A girl!" she squealed. She raced back in. "Family photo!"

Gerta quickly cleaned the baby while Clara adjusted Tina's blankets. Gerta passed the swaddled infant back to Tina, and she and George looked into their daughter's face for the first time.

"She's so tiny," Tina whispered.

"She has dark hair," George noticed.

Lisa clicked a few photos, and Clara called Santa and Walter in.

"Is that my granddaughter?" Santa asked in a hushed tone.

"Can I hold her?" Clara asked.

"I wish she would open her eyes." Tina handed her

to George. He gently cradled her and carefully walked over to Clara.

"She's tired. It's not easy being born." Clara took her and gazed at her with Santa.

Lisa leaned in to take a photo and continued snapping pictures until everyone grumbled about it.

"You'll thank me later." Lisa set the camera down on the dresser.

"Everyone out," Gerta ordered. "We must leave the parents alone so Tina can feed the baby."

Lisa turned back. "What's her name?"

Tina caught George's eyes. "We decided on Katina Gertrude. Gertrude was supposed to be the first Santa, and Katina was her daughter. I wanted to honor them."

"Well done." Santa smiled proudly as everyone filed out and shut the door.

"We can't call her Tina," George said.

Tina gazed down at the baby in her arms and Katina blinked at her.

"I want to call her Kate or Katie."

George tenderly kissed Katina's forehead. "Hello, beautiful Katie."

Tina unwrapped the blanket a bit. "Look at her little fingers and tiny fingernails."

"So perfect," George said in awe.

Katie opened her eyes and appeared to squint at them. Her eyes were deep blue.

"Welcome to the family, Katie," George said softly.

35 *A Favor*

"Nick!" Tina screamed into the phone. "You're an uncle. I had the baby."

"I thought you weren't going to have it until next month." He rubbed his eyes and meandered into his kitchen still groggy.

"She came early," Tina said. "I wonder if it had to do with all the stress of the storm."

"What storm?"

"Remember, they predicted a huge storm here?"

"No."

"Every fifty years or so, there's a big storm here and Gerta said it was coming this month. Blitzen told me the same thing," she explained. "Anyway, the power went out and the barn door came off and some windows broke."

"Sounds wild."

"Fritz got buried in the snow, but he's okay."

"Wild."

"You're an uncle!" she squealed. "Her name is Katina Gertrude, after the first chosen Santa and her daughter."

"But those are girl's names."

"Nick! Don't you remember the family history?" Tina demanded impatiently. "The first Santa was supposed to be a woman named Gertrude, but she was poisoned. They never found out who did it."

"Right."

"And her daughter was named Katina, so that's the baby's name, but we're going to call her Kate or Katie."

"Right."

"Oh, Nick. She's so tiny and cute and perfect," Tina gushed. "She has dark hair and dark blue eyes. Lisa took a ton of pictures. I'll tell her to text you one."

"Hey, congrats. Tell George congrats."

"Thanks." Tina felt tears welling in her eyes again. "I'm so wiped out, but so happy."

"You know I love you guys," Nick said.

"We love you too. Oh, I wish you were here," Tina cried. "I can't wait till you see her."

"Next month."

"Yes, we'll be back in Florida, but in the meantime, I have another delivery to get through and I feel so drained. I don't know how I'll do it."

"Then don't."

"I have to..."

"No, you don't. Dad's there."

Tina sighed. "Mom has been bugging me all year about this."

"So let Dad do it," Nick advised. "He's into it."

"I can't believe I'm considering this, but it makes total sense. I don't really feel up to it. It takes so much out of me. I was worried about doing it pregnant, but I was still going to do it."

"Right. But you don't have to."

"Nick, I'm so glad you're my brother."

"You made me an uncle, Tina. What am I going to do with a niece?"

"You're going to be the coolest uncle ever."

Tina wandered into the bedroom with her phone and peeked at Katina in the wooden cradle that Jann had made for her. She was sleeping peacefully, and Tina's heart was bursting with happiness and love.

"Oh, have you heard from Isabella?" she asked Nick.

"Yeah. She called and said she misses me." He chuckled. "She's crazy about me."

"And you're crazy about her."

"Guess so."

"I think next year is going to be a wonderful year," Tina said as Katina stirred.

"Me too," Nick responded.

***

Tina could hear Clara and George making dinner in the kitchen. Tantalizing smells wafted out, and she realized how hungry she was.

"You have a full tummy, don't you?" Santa cooed to Katina. He held her up to his shoulder and patted her back. "There you go. That's better, isn't it?"

He held her in his arms as she drifted off to sleep. He picked up the remote and lowered the volume on the TV. Tina had never seen him act so tenderly before. It was touching.

She sat on the couch beside him. "Dad." She smiled. "Grandpa."

Surprise flickered across his face for an instant. "She looks just like you did. Except for the hair."

"She does?" Tina asked, pleased to hear this.

"You were a little bigger because you were late."

Tina nodded. "Dad. I want to ask you a favor."

"I don't mind holding her."

"I know." Tina took a deep breath. "Will you guide the sleigh tomorrow night?"

Santa glanced at her with a frown. Clara had come out of the kitchen and stood drying her hands on a towel. George went over and stood beside her.

"Sorry. I couldn't resist." Tina gave a little laugh. "But seriously, I don't feel up to it. I mean, I could probably do it if I had to, but..."

"You should be here," Santa said decisively. "With Katina. And George."

"So you'll cover for me?" Tina asked.

Santa scratched his beard. "That's what we're here for. To pitch in. It's been a few years, but I suppose I could do it. Like riding a bike, right?"

"Thanks, Dad." Tina looked at her mother, who clutched the towel to her chest as she beamed at them.

"Uh oh. She's wet." Santa held the baby out.

"I'll change her." Clara took her from Santa.

George nodded at Tina and went back into the kitchen. Tina leaned over and kissed her father on his bristly cheek. He turned up the volume on the TV and without looking at her, patted her knee.

***

"It's too cold," George said with concern.

"She's fine. She's a Claus," Tina said. "We'll only be outside for a few minutes."

They were in the baking kitchen by the back door of the building. Jars of candy canes lined the shelves along with freshly baked gingerbread houses. Tina breathed in the familiar aroma. It was a tradition to send them home with the elves. Everyone had worked so hard this year to catch up after the storm had set them back. But it had all come together. The elves would return in the next few days to help shut down for the season and to collect their gingerbread houses and candy canes.

"Do you want me to get you a chair?" George asked.

"No, I'm fine."

George pushed open the door, and they carefully stepped outside into the brisk chill of the evening to join Clara, Walter, and Lisa.

"The suit is loose on him since he lost weight," Walter observed.

"He had to tighten his belt," Clara said. "Oh, but look at him." She clasped her hands together in delight.

The reindeer snorted impatiently, jostling each other. The red sleigh was loaded with presents. How could all those presents fit into one sleigh? Christmas magic. Santa removed his glove and patted each reindeer with great fondness. Tina had watched him do this many times. And now she knew how it felt. She longed to get into the sleigh herself and feel that upward whoosh, but she looked down in her arms and was perfectly content to stay right here on the ground this one time.

Blitzen nodded to Tina, and she smiled. She approached the reindeer and let them admire the baby. They nodded their huge heads and Katina received a few affectionate licks on her cheek. She fussed a bit before settling back to sleep. Tina stepped back with George and watched her father climb into the sleigh.

"The new seat feels good," Santa called to her. "Okay, here we go."

The reindeer pawed the ground before slowly taking those first steps forward, tugging at the sleigh before it began to glide behind them. The frozen snow crunched under their hooves as they trotted.

"Now, Blitzen and Donner. And Comet and Cupid. And Dasher and Dancer. And Prancer and Vixen and Rudolph. Dash away! Dash away!" Santa bellowed.

"That's your grandpa," Tina said in Katina's ear, rocking her in her arms. "And next year you'll watch Mommy."

The reindeer broke into a brisk gallop, shaking the ground beneath them. With a sparkly burst, they rose into the velvety night sky. Tina knew what it felt like to suddenly sail above the ground with the wind pushing the sleigh up. She would get her chance again next year. And the next. And the next. And as long as she was able.

"I used to put a movie on TV and give you and Nick popcorn," Clara shared. "Do you remember? I couldn't let you watch when you were little because you used to get upset seeing your father leave."

Tina nodded. "We used to watch out the window, anyway."

But she had a memory of running through the kitchen one dark night crying for her father. She'd felt scared and abandoned. She hadn't understood why he was flying off. And now here she was, watching him one last time and feeling the joy and magic of this exhilarating moment.

"Let me take the baby inside." Clara reached out and Tina handed her over.

"It's freezing out here." Lisa hurried inside, with Walter right behind her.

George put his arm around Tina. It was a clear night and they could still see Santa rising higher into the darkness.

"Ho! Ho! Ho!" Santa's voice rang out as he disappeared from sight.

"Is that what I look like?" Tina's face was tilted up to the spattering of stars and the glowing moon.

"Pretty much." George started for the door.

Tina turned toward the building and entered the door that he held open. Everyone had gone upstairs, and they stood alone in the kitchen. Tina peeked out the window.

"There's not a word for how cold it is," George said, removing his gloves.

Tina felt tears in her eyes and smiled at him. "There's not a word for how happy I am. My heart is full."

"Mine is fuller." He grinned. "Let's go upstairs and sit by the fire and have hot chocolate."

"Do we have mini marshmallows?"

"Have I ever let you down?" He raised his eyebrows.

"Never." Tina wiped her eyes with her glove. "These gingerbread houses smell so good."

"Can we bring one upstairs?" George asked.

"Sure. There's always one for us."

"It's nice to have you here tonight." George pulled her close and kissed her.

"What a year it's been," Tina marveled. "Every year gets better. I don't see how we can top this one."

"There's always the next baby." He grinned.

"Hold on," Tina said. "Baby number two is going to have to wait. In fact, I think you should have the next one."

"Gladly." George turned his attention to choosing a gingerbread house.

Tina gazed out the window again. The snow shimmered in the pale light of the moon, and she thought she detected a twinkle in the air. The barn was empty, and the season was over. It had all come together brilliantly. And there would be many more seasons. And more challenges. And more love and joy and happiness. And another generation to carry on the Claus tradition.

***

From the Author

I hope you enjoyed **The More the Merrier**, the last book in the Santina Series! Clara is named after my mother, who gave me the original story idea. I never expected to continue writing the Claus family's story, but they stayed with me after the first book. Thanks for spending time with the lovable Claus family! And if you want more, be sure to read the free prequel, **The Santa Secret** about how Santa and Clara met and fell in love.

If you enjoyed this book, please post a rating or brief review on Amazon and/or Goodreads. I appreciate every one and it helps readers decide whether to read this book. Thank you!

Be sure to read the free prequel **The Santa Secret** if you missed it! The description is on the next page. Or read **Fairy Tale Karma** next! The description and first chapter are on the following pages.

Each of my novels explores family and friendship, love and romance, and relationships and life. All are available on Amazon and free to read through Kindle Unlimited. Follow me on Amazon, BookBub, and Goodreads, where you can read my blog.

~*~*~*~*~*~*~*~*~*~*~

The Santa Secret (Prequel)

Ho, Ho, Huh?

When Clara meets and falls in love with Nicky, she has no clue who he is. He says he's going to inherit the family business up north, but little does she know it's at the North Pole. Then Nicky claims he's going to be the next Santa when his father retires. And she can never tell anyone. Ever.

Clara is used to life in balmy Florida. If she wants to be with Nicky, they'll have to live at the frigid North Pole. With his parents. And talking reindeer, walking snowmen, and elves. What has Clara gotten herself into?

Join the Claus family for Christmas magic, a whirlwind romance, a sleigh full of fun, and a whole lot of heart in this standalone merry prequel to the Santina Series!

Fairy Tale Karma

Ava married her Prince Charming, and they lived happily ever after. Or did they?

Princess Ava is interviewed by a skeptical journalist digging for the truth behind the fairy tale, but she defends the myth by relating an idealized storybook version while we find out the truth in flashbacks. Young Ava's mother runs off with another man, and her clueless father marries a heartless woman who makes Ava toil as a maid at her inn. All the while, Ava dreams of living in that beautiful castle in the distance. Enter her newly sober Fairy Godmother, who promises to help her achieve her wish. But her unstable magic and the arrival of an irresistible guy at the inn threaten their plans. How will Ava fulfill her destiny? And then what?

Things don't quite turn out as she imagines. Her handsome prince is always distracted by charity work while she gets hooked on romance novels. What an ironic twist of fate! Their therapist certainly has his work cut out for him! Can this marriage be saved?

The past and present collide in this funny, romantic, magical fantasy story based on Cinderella that will make you believe in fairy tales!

"The last decent Cinderella adaptation I read was Ella Enchanted *by Gail Carson Levine, and that book was written in 1998! Here is the newsflash Ms. Thrush gives: you can't ever outgrow fairy tales!" Kelly Smith Reviews*

"Very funny read. Like a version of a twisted fairy tale. So clever... Gotta love the drunken fairy godmother who was banned from the castle! Hard to put down once I started reading." Autism Mom

"...filled with magic and imagination... I loved the twists and turns." Judy Hall Jacobson

"Surprisingly insightful: Not your average fluff tale... I liked this story but I wasn't ready for it to be so thought-provoking." BBomm

Enjoy the first chapter next!

1 ~*Happily Ever After?*~

Jill wondered if she'd made a mistake. Why had she worked so hard to convince her editor to let her go on this puff-piece assignment? After all, she was an investigative journalist. What had possessed her to pursue such a trivial story? Yet something had nagged at her until she could no longer ignore it, though now it just seemed frivolous. Still, the Princess was expecting her, so she had to follow through. She was annoyed with herself and hoped her instincts hadn't failed her.

She'd driven a long way in her rental car to find the little hamlet tucked away in a hidden valley protected by rolling hills. Far from congested freeways, she passed through fields and dales, loops and hills, aiming for what was over the horizon ahead.

Her goal was to do the interview quickly and return home to dash off the piece, exposing the Princess's fabrications. There was no such thing as happily ever after, and she intended to prove it, so that young girls would no longer fall prey to these silly fantasies and could get on with their lives. Once this was out of her system, she'd resume her career with more serious reporting. That was the plan.

Jill rounded the bend in the road that would lead into the center of the town of Quimby in the commonwealth territory of Wellstonia. What she saw made her pull over, and she rummaged in her oversized bag for her camera and opened the car door.

It was as if someone had painted this idyllic scene. A glistening white castle stood off to one side while the butter-yellow sun illuminated the town in a warm golden glow. A vivid rainbow stretched across the sky as birds chirped in the verdant trees. A feeling of joy washed over her. It was as if her dreams had painted this perfect picture. She felt as if she'd stepped into a storybook.

~~~

Princess Ava glanced at the grandfather clock. She had her doubts about agreeing to this interview. What if this reporter discerned the truth? Not to mention, there was an unspoken rule of discretion among royals. The Prince would surely be displeased, but that wasn't her primary concern. Her attire was more important at the moment. She'd chosen a lovely cream-colored gown and a small tiara to greet her visitor. After all, she was a princess. How fun to dress up and impress someone from the outside.

Footsteps echoed from the hallway. The castle was vast and drafty, and the acoustics were terribly annoying. She stood and waited, striking a regal pose. Despite her tiny reservations, she was looking forward to sharing her famous story. It was a tremendous responsibility to set the bar for romance, and she took it seriously.

Sarah, one of the staff, entered with a young woman trailing her. The woman's hair was long and dark. She wore glasses and had a large fabric bag slung over her shoulder. She approached with an extended hand and quickly withdrew it with embarrassment.

"May I present Jill Graham, Princess," Sarah intoned.

"Your Highness, I'm not sure of the protocol." Jill appeared flustered.

Princess Ava smiled graciously and sat on a floral couch. "Don't worry about it. Have a seat. Just make yourself comfortable." She looked at Sarah. "We'll have some tea and pastries. Thank you."

Sarah nodded and exited.

"Thank you." Jill seated herself on a matching couch opposite Princess Ava. "Please tell me if I do anything inappropriate. I'm not familiar with the protocol."

"Please don't worry about all that. I've never given an exclusive interview, so this is a first for both of us."
~~~

She smiled to put Jill at ease.

"Okay." Jill seemed to relax a bit.

She studied the Princess, who was flawlessly beautiful, with perfect smooth skin and silky blonde hair. Jewels and gems dripped from her, and her necklace shimmered with a rainbow of colors, as did her earrings and matching bracelet. Rings adorned almost all of her fingers.

"Why don't we begin with some background information?" Jill suggested.

"Such as?" Princess Ava asked. "Everyone already knows my story. Poor girl meets the Prince. We fall madly in love and live happily ever after. End of story." She leaned forward, and her soft blonde curls fell in her face. She brushed them back with a delicate hand. "I'm curious about why you contacted me for an interview. No one has ever asked for an interview before."

"Well, Princess, I want to know if that *is* the end of the story." Jill pulled a notepad and pen from her bag. "Girls of all ages all over the world want to know what it's like living with a prince. Can you really live happily ever after? I think there's more to the story."

Princess Ava looked toward one of the tall windows framed by long drapes. Sunlight streamed in, spilling onto the thick carpet.

"Has my story given people hope?"

"It depends," Jill answered.

Somewhere inside her was a shred of optimism that life could turn out happily ever after. She wanted so much to believe as she had when she was younger, but reality had callously squashed that dream under its heel.

Princess Ava's light blue eyes stared into Jill's dark brown ones. "Depends on what?"

"The truth," Jill stated simply.

Sarah entered, carrying a silver tray that she set on the coffee table between them. Upon the tray were a small teapot and two white teacups with saucers. Flaky pastries and an assortment of cookies were arranged on a plate with two smaller plates beside it. She stood attentively.

"Thank you, Sarah." Princess Ava nodded at her and she quietly left.

Jill suddenly realized she was hungry after her long drive. She'd snacked in the car, as she often did at her desk while she worked.

"Are you married?" Princess Ava asked as she reached for a cookie.

"Divorced." Jill placed a pastry on one of the smaller plates.

Princess Ava nodded and leaned back. "Now you're disillusioned."

"I think I'm more realistic."

Her mind raced with questions. There was so much to cover. She hoped to meet the Prince and tour the castle and the grounds. Then she remembered to get out her recorder. She pulled it from her bag.

"Do you mind, Princess?"

Princess Ava waved her hand. "Not at all."

Jill set the small device on the coffee table beside the tray and clicked it on as she took a bite of the pastry. It was divine, so light, it melted in her mouth.

Princess Ava smiled. "It's irresistible, isn't it? The best in the land."

"Yes, delicious." She delved into the interview as soon as she finished chewing. "So, is the story true? Were you a poor, abused girl forced into manual labor by your stepmother until your fairy godmother helped you meet the Prince?"

"Absolutely. The gist of it is true. We were poor. I had few options in life." Princess Ave shook her head at the memory. "I used to look out my window at the castle and wonder what it'd be like to live in this beautiful palace."

Jill looked at the notepad on which she'd scribbled questions. "Tell me about your parents. Your bio says that your mother died and your father remarried. Your stepmother favored her own children and treated you like a servant. Is that true?" She gave the Princess a sympathetic look.

"I came home from school one day and my mother was gone," Princess Ava related. "I remember walking home from school. It was a beautiful day, like today. There were some people standing on the steps of The Sleep Inn. They stopped talking and watched me as I walked by. I could tell something was wrong, so I ran the rest of the way home."

"That must've been difficult," Jill commented. "It's terrible for a girl to lose her mother."

"My mother was too young to wither away in this little town," Princess Ava intoned. "I mean to say, she was too young to die. She was pretty and smart and ambitious." She cleared her throat. "I mean, she could've done anything."

"Your father must've been devastated," Jill whispered.

"I think my father was in shock for a long time. We both felt lost without her."

"Understandably so. Didn't he remarry right away, so you'd have a mother?"

"Hazel ran The Sleep Inn. She'd lost her husband, and I guess she thought they could help each other," Princess Ava explained.

Jill reached for another pastry. She took a small bite. "Mmm. These are unbelievably good."

Princess Ava reached for one. "Aren't they? I have to be careful not to eat too many. The food here is so good." She poured two cups of tea. "Where was I?"

"You were telling me about your stepmother," Jill reminded her.

"Yes. I don't believe Hazel ever loved my father. I think she just wanted help with the inn. I had to do all the housekeeping. It was a lot of work, so much so, that I had to quit school." Princess Ava shook her head. "My father just never stood up to her. He spent most of his time at work."

"That's terrible," Jill responded. "What kind of work

did your father do?"

"He was a bookkeeper. His major client was a dentist. That's why I have such nice teeth. He was always reminding me to floss." She opened her mouth to show off her teeth.

"You do have beautiful teeth," Jill agreed. "What else can you tell me about that difficult time?"

Princess Ava leaned forward. "That's when I realized I have a special gift," she confided. "Some people thought I was crazy, but that word is so subjective, isn't it? I'm just as sane as you are."

"I'm sure you are. And what is this gift?" Jill reached for her cup of tea.

"You have to understand something about this place. It's different. You can feel it in the air. Do you feel it?"

"Feel what?"

Princess Ava smiled and leaned back. "Magic. This place is enchanted. It's all around us. My gift isn't really that unusual in a place like this."

"Okay," Jill said slowly.

"The story is true. I can communicate with animals. The birds and other small animals were my friends and helped me get through the rough times until I met Agnes," Princess Ava asserted. "I know it sounds far-fetched, but remember where we are."

"Okay. So, the animals were your friends and looked out for you. Now who is Agnes?"

"Agnes is my fairy godmother."

Jill grabbed her notepad and pen. Things were getting interesting.

"So, Agnes is the one who made it all happen. How did she appear to you?"

"I wish you could've seen her. She floated toward me in a sparkling bubble of light. She was the most beautiful thing I'd ever seen."

"Wow." Jill tried to imagine such an extraordinary sight.

"Agnes came along in my deepest moment of

despair. She saw the grief and pain inside my heart. She knew what my destiny was and revealed it to me, and I cried with joy." Princess Ava dabbed at her eye with a napkin.

"How did she help you meet the Prince?" Jill asked. "Is it true that he took one look at you, fell instantly in love, and then searched all over for you?"

"Of course, it's all true," Princess Ava said.

Jill checked the recorder. "Go on. Then what happened?"

"Agnes saw my dreadful situation and vowed to help me. She knew that the Prince and I were meant to be together. She told me she would convince the King and Queen to host a royal ball to find a match for the Prince."

"And that's how you met."

"It was our one chance to fulfill our romantic destiny." Princess Ava sighed.

~~~
~~~

May your life be filled with great books!

Made in the USA
Monee, IL
08 July 2026